I0186911

FOLLOW
THE
INSTRUCTIONS

Follow the Instructions

By

Jenabe E. Caldwell

Best Publisher
Wailuku, Hawaii

http://www.jenabe.org

Follow the Instructions

Published by Best Publisher
Wailuku, Hawaii

http://www.jenabe.net

©Jenabe E. Caldwell
All rights reserved

Fourth Edition 2008

ISBN: 0-9762780-6-5

CONTENTS

Forward vii

Chapter 1   The Supreme Command 1

Chapter 2   A Little Child shall Lead Them 5

Chapter 3   A Sublime Station 11

Chapter 4   Unholy Competition 15

Chapter 5   Listen with Heart and Soul 21

Chapter 6   Prayer and Inspiration 27

Chapter 7   Follow Your Heart 35

Chapter 8   Foundation of All Human Virtues 43

Chapter 9   Tender Loving Care (TLC) 45

Chapter 10 Divine Education 49

Chapter 11 Pick and Choose 55

Chapter 12 Obey the Laws 59

Chapter 13 Live the Life and Serve 61

Chapter 14 The Mystery of Sacrifice 67

Chapter 15 The Greatest Gift 75

Chapter 16 Love Comes from Bahá'u'lláh 87

Chapter 17 Teach Every Stratum 99

Chapter 18 Cultural Diversity 111

Chapter 19 O God! Give Me Wisdom 115

Chapter 20 My Calamity is My Providence 119

Chapter 21 With Fire We Test the Gold 131

Chapter 22 The Power of Prayer 137

Chapter 23 Don't Be in A Hurry 143

Chapter 24 Soy Bahá'í 147

Chapter 25 Hi-Jacking 153

Chapter 26 Jamal Effendi 159

Abbreviations of Book Titles 163

FORWARD

This small book is being written for Bahá'í teachers in the hope that it will make their individual and group teaching easier and more productive. Although most of the stories related are from my personal experience, some of them are from other Bahá'í teachers, and were told to me by them. All the incidents in this book are true. The stories told to me were confirmed by other eye witnesses. When the teachers would come in from the teaching field, we would have a de-briefing. The things that happened that day would be shared with the whole team. Some of the details would be supplied by other members of the team. In the morning before the teams would depart for the day's work, we would have a briefing. Often the consultation would be determined by what we learned from the de-briefing from the day before. Many times more details would be given about the incidents at the briefing.

Pioneers are mentioned in the book and these were and are people that move to another place to make their home, find work and teach the Cause of God.

Every year from April 21 until May 2 is a period that we call Riḍván. It was the time that Bahá'u'lláh was leaving Baghdád. Bahá'u'lláh at that time made His declaration to His close friends. Every year during this period the Bahá'í's of the world elect their Local Spiritual Assemblies. These Local Spiritual Assemblies are elected by secret ballot and consist of nine members.

The Bahá'í teaching teams that are referred to in the book are groups of Bahá'ís that go out teaching together. The teams I worked with consisted of a minimum of five up to as many as one hundred and fifty. The training sessions referred to were from 9 days to 14 days in length called institutes. This was preparation for us to learn about the instructions and try to follow them in a real world with real people.

The Tablet of Ahmad is a Bahá'í prayer that was revealed in Arabic around 1865. The Guardian, Shoghi Effendi said in Bahá'í prayers page-209 that this particular prayer was invested by Bahá'u'lláh with a special potency and significance. In this book you will find that we used it with great success.

This book is dedicated to that God intoxicated army of Bahá'u'lláh, the front line teachers of His Cause.

CHAPTER 1

THE SUPREME COMMAND

Bahá'u'lláh

Instruction :

"O My Servant! Obey Me and I shall make thee like unto Myself. . ."

FV-63

Many people ask me, "What is the secret of success in teaching one to one or mass teaching in large groups?" The answer is the same. **"Just follow the instructions."** When everything else fails, re-read the instructions, and to the best of your ability try to follow them. In the army of light we have a Supreme Command. It is **Bahá'u'lláh, `Abdu'l-Bahá, Shoghi Effendi** and the **Universal House of Justice.** Under the Supreme Command are the Generals of Bahá'u'lláh's Army of Light, the National Spiritual Assemblies and the Continental Boards of Councillor. This must include the whole Administrative Order.

Bahá'u'lláh

Instruction :

"Be unrestrained as the wind, while carrying the Message of Him Who hath caused the Dawn of Divine Guidance to break. Consider, how the wind, faithful to that which God hath ordained, bloweth upon all regions of the earth, be they inhabited or desolate."

Gl-339

In most of our teaching, one must learn early on to be very flexible and cast nothing in concrete. We have our plans and God has His and we must learn to do it His way. Except, of course, for the instructions of the Supreme Command, which are truly cast in concrete, and violation of them is to court disaster. We must also try to follow the instructions of those God intoxicated Generals of Bahá'u'lláh's army, the National Spiritual Assemblies. If one finds that these instructions do not work, or are not based on a real life situation, then it is necessary to go back to the National Spiritual Assembly and through loving consultation, get new and workable instructions.

Shoghi Effendi

Instruction :

> ". . . *the authority of the National Spiritual Assembly is undivided and unchallengeable in all matters pertaining to the administration of the Faith . . . and that, therefore, the obedience of individual Bahá'ís . . . is imperative, and should be whole-hearted and unqualified.*"

LG-36

About 25 years ago, I was teaching in Central America and ran into a National Spiritual Assembly with some horrendous problems. I sat down and documented all the problems and fired off this information to the Universal House of Justice. The reply was that they were well aware of the situation and that it was true, but the best way to help that immature National Spiritual Assembly into maturity was by loving obedience.

These two words have since carried me around the world, and have helped me in working with 62 National

Spiritual Assemblies in many different climes and cultures. We must come to realize that to help these administrative bodies into maturity can be of greater and more lasting service than the enrolling of thousands of new Bahá'ís.

Loving obedience does not mean grudgingly, with deep-seated reservations, and a feeling that you will do it even though you think it may be the wrong decision. Loving obedience means that you are sure the instruction has come from Bahá'u'lláh Himself through the National Spiritual Assembly and you are excited and ready to give it your all.

Sometimes, however, the instructions for you seem to violate your conscience. In that rare instance, if your heartfelt consultation with the Administration does not satisfy your conscience, you should just go home and send money for the work of the Cause. One thing to remember and constantly remind ourselves is that, we need the Cause of God; it does not need us. We are allowed the priceless privilege of serving Him.

Bahá'u'lláh

Instruction :

> *"The prophets of God should be regarded as physicians whose task is to foster the well-being of the world and its peoples, that, through the spirit of oneness, they may heal the sickness of a divided humanity."*

Gl-80

Bahá'u'lláh is the Divine Physician and He is operating on the sick body of mankind. He picks up a scalpel (the Bahá'í teacher) and if it is clean and usable, He uses it. If not, He drops it into the autoclave for further sterilizing and sharpening. He then picks up another scalpel and goes on with the operation. O God! Please don't let me throw myself in the garbage. Just remember that Bahá'u'lláh is the Supreme Commander and He is directing this dramatic engagement from His retreats of Glory.

CHAPTER 2

A LITTLE CHILD SHALL LEAD THEM

Bahá'u'lláh

Instruction :

*"Let them,'proclaim that which the Most
Great Spirit will inspire them to utter in
the service of the Cause of their Lord.' "*

ADJ-50

It was in South Carolina, the city was Charleston, and
the time was during the mass teaching in the late 1960's.
Because it was on a Sunday the entire teaching team was
going out to do street teaching. This means meeting people
in the park or on the streets and giving them a courteous and
loving invitation to our meeting. If they respond in a positive
manner, then we were to share with them the message of
Bahá'u'lláh. As you may know, Charleston is a large city
with many parks and places that lend themselves well to this
type of teaching.

Shoghi Effendi

Instruction :

*". . .audacity in teaching is essential,
but no less important is the necessity for
the exercise of the utmost tact, wisdom,
and consideration, in either separate
individuals or large public audiences."*

LG-600

There were five teachers in this one car and even with such a small group, a team leader was put in charge. All teams were advised that they must not hassle the leader. This was done to avoid the bickering and wrangling over such fruitless conversations as whether to having bananas or oranges for lunch. Also, if you have five people deciding where to go, you will end up with five totally different ideas. You will end up with everyone upset, and not in the proper mood for teaching. You must understand that we had a lot of time in the morning after dawn prayers to consult on everything, from living problems to the teaching. We had learned through the school of hard knocks that in the field, and especially on the streets, are not the proper places for consultation that, in most cases, can become the "clash of differing opinions." This is not at all understood by the general population that watches the show.

Bahá'u'lláh

Instruction :

> *"Conflict and contention are categorically forbidden in His Book. This is a decree of God in this Most Great Revelation. It is divinely preserved from annulment and is invested by Him with the splendour of His confirmation."*

TB-221

These teachers were further instructed that, if they did not agree with the team leader, the best way to help him or her in making a better decision was to ask for prayers, which all team members were encouraged to do, not only for problems but to help maintain the spiritual atmosphere so needed to sustain the daily teaching effort.

So this team leader instructed the driver of the car to
turn here, turn there and was taking this team right down
into the very heart of the industrial area of Charleston on
Sunday. The area of factories, chain link fences and empty
parking lots. Someone suggested that they say prayers and
all said nine remover of difficulties. The leader then said,
"OK, stop the car." The car pulled over to the curb and
stopped on a deserted street. Someone suggested that they
say a round of "Tablets of Aḥmad." Which they did, and the
team leader then said, "OK, everybody out of the car, let's
go teach." If I had been there, I am sure I would have not
been able to keep silent, but this group was made of better
stuff. They all got out of the car and as there were no
people at all on the street, they all tagged along with their
leader. When they went around the corner, they saw a small
child of four or five-years old playing on the sidewalk. The
team leader walked up to this child and said, "Do you
know that your Lord and Savior Jesus Christ has come
back?"

This little black child looked at the team leader and
pointed up to the sky and said, "You mean that Jesus?"

The team leader said, "Yes."

The baby jumped up and grabbed the team leader's
hand and shouted, "Come let's go tell grandma." They
rushed in behind one of the closed and quiet factories,
up the stairs and into an apartment, with the child pulling
the team leader by the hand, the other team members
following. Sitting in a rocking chair was a very old white
haired lady, and the baby rushed up to her and all excited
shouted, "Grandma, Grandma, Jesus has come back! Jesus
has come back!"

This old woman looked at those spiritually radiant faces,
who had just said five Tablets of Aḥmad that God would

guide them, smiled, nodded her head and said, "I know this is true."

The leader replied, "Lady, how do you know this is true?"

"Well son," she said; "Didn't the Good Book say that a little child will lead them and didn't this baby just lead you in here?"

There were 15 adults and some children in that apartment and all of them became Bahá'ís. All these people were just getting ready to split for the day to different places and different preoccupations. This team, following another instruction right out of the Kitáb-i-Aqdas, **"To respond to invitations" (KA-161)**, stayed for Sunday dinner with that family, spent the whole day and evening with them, and were able to do fantastic consolidation. Again then: **Bahá'u'lláh is the Supreme Commander and He is directing this dramatic engagement from His retreats of Glory.**

This story points out also the spirit of patience and tolerance that the teachers must have for their companions. So often the teachers lose sight of another attribute and that is courtesy. Not only must we be the very essence of courtesy to those we are trying to teach but we must also practice this virtue with each other.

Bahá'u'lláh

Instruction :

> *"Adorn. . . your bodies with the vesture of courtesy."*

KA- K120

For example, you have a teacher talking to a person, and in following the instruction to listen, asks a question, before the person being taught has a chance to even think about an answer, another teacher immediately butts in and takes over the fireside. This is one of the great ego trips where you think that you are the only one who can supply the right answer.

Bahá'u'lláh

Instruction :

> *"To none is it permitted to mutter sacred verses before the public gaze as he walketh in the street or marketplace";*
>
> *KA-K108*

When someone is teaching, the best advice is for you to find someone else to teach. If you can't then the best help you can give to the teaching work is to silently and in your heart pray for the one that is talking that he or she may be guided to touch the heart of the one being taught. Never, never, never interrupt or butt into someone else's conversation. When you pray on the streets, it must be done only in that most private of chambers, which is the human heart.

CHAPTER 3

A SUBLIME STATION

Bahá'u'lláh

Instruction :

> *"O people of God! I admonish you to observe courtesy. For above all else it is the prince of virtues. Well is it with him who is illumined with the light of courtesy and is attired with the vesture of uprightness. Whoso is endued with courtesy hath indeed attained a sublime station."*

TB-88

This can be better understood by an incident that took place during the mass teaching campaign in Guyana. The teachers had spent much time in preparation, and this principle of courtesy was talked about and understood by all members of the teaching team. When one talked the others silently prayed and as a result we were enrolling a large number of receptive souls. One of these newly found Bahá'ís was a Moslem woman and her children. Her husband, however, was the son of the local Mullah and when any member of the team tried to talk to him he excused himself and ran away.

Universal House of Justice

Instruction :

> *"After declaration, the new believers must not be left to their own devices."*

WG-32

As we were staying with the new found friends and were not leaving them to their own devices, but were diligently working night and day to consolidate them we visited this woman almost daily. She was a most sincere and beautiful soul, and we also had children's classes for her children. Her husband also was a very sweet and beautiful soul and we all longed to make this whole family Bahá'í.

One day, I was sitting on the steps with her husband. Some of the other team members were doing the children's class and I was talking about this, that and the other thing with him. I knew that if I tried to talk about the Faith he would run away. Up comes a Buddhist priest, and he began to ask me questions about the Faith. It was obvious that he just wanted to talk and was not really interested. "What a God given opportunity," I thought. I began to tell the Buddhist about the Cause of God from the stand point of the Qur'án and the Moslems and because this husband did not feel threatened, he was all ears and for the first time was listening. One of the other teachers with me who had come from a Buddhist background, who had no idea of what I was doing, went and found one of our teachers, (who had been a Buddhist priest), interrupted me and said, "Excuse me Jenabe but I am sure you are not answering this man's questions and I am sure this former priest can do a better job." Of course I shut up, and in a few minutes the woman's husband who was not at all interested in that approach, left and we were never given another chance with him. I was right the Buddhist priest was not really interested.

'Abdu'l-Bahá

Instruction :

> *"The teacher should not consider himself as learned and others ignorant. Such a thought breedeth pride, and pride is not conducive to influence."*

SAB-30

There is another side to this coin and that is we must be alert to the fact that we can't always get on the same wave length as the person we are trying to teach and must therefore be wise enough to recognize this and turn our contact over to another teacher as soon as we find we are not getting through. When I was traveling with Amátu'l-Bahá Rúhíyyih Khánum in Alaska she gave a most beautiful public talk and when she finished she said to the chairman, "Now you tell them." The chairman protested and Amátu'l-Bahá Rúhíyyih Khánum told him that there were people there she could not reach and that he should tell them. He did, and when he finished Amátu'l-Bahá Rúhíyyih Khánum said, "Now everyone knows."

The Massive Encounter was a teaching project of the National Spiritual Assembly of Alaska during the late 1960's and early 1970's. They had decided to try to reach and teach every soul in Alaska. With a minimum goal of letting everyone know that Bahá'u'lláh came and give them an opportunity to accept or reject His message.

In Alaska, during massive encounter we once had six or seven different teachers each try, without any success, to reach one soul. Yet the last person to try, in just a few minutes was heart to heart with this person and we had a new Bahá'í.

It seems to be human nature that we don't like to admit defeat, and if we are defeated we don't like to see someone else succeed where we failed. This thinking is old world and is just another ego trip that we must recognize. After all, our sole purpose is to rescue a sick and disillusioned humanity and bring them all safely aboard Bahá'u'lláh's Crimson Ark. We must strive with heart and soul toward this end and aid one another in this work.

CHAPTER 4

UNHOLY COMPETITION

Universal House of Justice

Instruction :

> *"Some teaching committees, in their eagerness to obtain results, place undue emphasis on obtaining a great number of declarations to the detriment of the quality of teaching."*

WG-35

It is well understood why the teacher must sign the enrollment card: so that any questions that the administration might have about the new Bahá'í can be followed up. In country after country and campaign after campaign we have seen this become a source of unholy competition. The teachers become careless in their teaching and even become card collectors instead of heart collectors. It is almost as if they think they will get gold stars in heaven for the cards they collect, or feathers in their caps. Nothing could be further from the truth. Whose teachings are they? Whose inspiration is it? Whose Holy Spirit is it? Whose Concourse on High is it? Whose angels rank upon rank and file upon file are they? Who guides us to those hearts that are prepared, and who guides them to us? There is only one answer, and that is a conclusive, "Bahá'u'lláh's." The teachers should write this on their hearts, or better still, brand this into their souls, and that is the quotation from the Valley of Unity by Bahá'u'lláh.

Bahá'u'lláh

Instruction :

*"He seeth in himself neither name nor
fame nor rank, but findeth his own praise
in praising God."*

SV-18

If credit must be given, then be truthful and give the
credit where the credit is due: in praise and thanks giving
to Bahá'u'lláh.

Universal House of Justice

Instruction :

*"Some traveling teachers, in their desire
to show the result of their services, may
not scrupulously teach their contacts, and
in some rare cases, if, God forbid, they
are insincere, may even give false
reports."*

WG-35

In one country, the National Spiritual Assembly asked
me to go to a village and check up on the Local Assembly
that had been formed by a travel teacher. I had the list of
a large community of Bahá'ís and the officers of this Local
Assembly. When I tried to find the Chairman I was informed
that he was dead, and when I tried to find the other members
I was informed that they were dead. So I went to the grave
yard and here I found the whole Bahá'í community, including
the entire Local Assembly, side by side and all united and
all doing the same thing together. This teacher, in order to
meet his so-called quota, had gone to the grave yard and
enrolled the new believers from the names on the tomb

stones. A truly remarkable Bahá'í community. Talk about a truly peaceful bunch of Bahá'ís.

Bahá'u'lláh

Instruction :

> *"He beholdeth in his own name the name of God; to Him all songs are from the King"*

> *SV-18*

If it is feathers you want in your cap think about this story: A man left home and went to a far off place. He soon wrote a letter to his wife and said he had just landed a fantastic job, "A feather in my cap." He sent no money. A few months later his wife got another letter saying he had been promoted to foreman, "A feather in my cap." Again he sent no money. Several months later the letter comes saying he was promoted to manager, "A feather in my cap." Still no money. Then a wire comes saying that he had lost his job, "Please send money to come home." The wife wires back, "Use feathers fly home." That is how much value you will get also if you are looking for feathers in your cap from service to the Cause.

Bahá'u'lláh

Instruction :

> *"He hath, moreover, ordained that His Cause be taught through the power of men's utterance, and not through resort to violence."*

> *GI-278*

This card collecting and forcing people to sign is one of the most devastating problems facing the field of mass teaching. During mass teaching in Taiwan, a beautiful Chinese Bahá'í who I had enrolled in the faith, (and even got to go out with the teaching team), became almost totally inactive because some of the mass teachers were putting the Chinese contacts in the position of losing face in front of these foreigners if they didn't sign. They knew if they did sign, they would lose face with their families. These teachers were putting these people between a rock and a hard spot.

In South Carolina during the mass teaching the call went out for the friends to come help. The response was great, and on that weekend 2500 cards were collected. I, as an Auxiliary Board Member was privileged to go visit these new friends. They told me that they thought they were signing up for a free magazine "The American Bahá'í," or they were asked if they believed in world peace and if they said yes they were asked to sign a card. We ended up, after that fiasco, with 25 new Bahá'ís out of the 2500. Which is not too bad for a week-end teaching project. Today I don't think we would lose so many. When the person would say that they thought they were getting a subscription for a magazine we would take that opportunity to teach them the Cause. It would take a long time and a lot of effort.

Bahá'u'lláh

Instruction :

> *"Be thou steadfast in the Cause, and teach the people with consummate wisdom."*

TB-16

In Korea during a mass teaching project some years ago the National Spiritual Assembly told me about an all Bahá'í village. A Persian had even built a Local Bahá'í center there but the only person in the whole village to vote was the man living at the center. They asked me to go with the Auxiliary Board Member and check it out. This Board member was a wonderful Bahá'í, but we got one of the coldest receptions I have ever gotten anywhere.

The people refused to even talk to us, but with perseverance we finally got one of the villagers to tell us the problem. It seems that the travel teacher that had enrolled the villagers, had promised the people that the National Spiritual Assembly would get them all lights and electricity for their homes. Here it was, a number of years later, and still no electricity.

With my translator we went house to house and explained that the lights they had received were the lights that would never go out and we very patiently taught that village the Cause of God. We formed the Local Assembly.

All the villagers came every morning for Dawn Prayers, and we started extension teaching in a nearby village. One day, the nine members of the Local Assembly explained that the following morning the men would have to go for their military service. I told them, "Never mind about missing dawn prayers as Bahá'u'lláh said that work is worship." They told me that instead of having the prayers at 6 AM, they would like, just this once to have them at 4 AM. Much later, when I was down in the southern tip of Korea, I got a letter from this Local Assembly signed by the Chairman. They had found the English words in a magazine, cut them out and pasted them on the letter. It said, "We will make our Local Assembly the best in Korea. Thank you." I was so thrilled with the letter that I forwarded it on to the Hand of the Cause of God, Dr. Rahmatu'llá Muhájir, who had sent me to Korea.

Pushing people to sign cards, and making them feel like second class citizens if they don't, only makes enemies for this Cause we love so much, and God knows we don't need any more enemies.

CHAPTER 5

LISTEN WITH HEART AND SOUL

The art of listening. Yes, it is an art, and like any artistic talent, the more you practice the better you get. When Bahá'u'lláh was sending Hájí Mírzá Haydar-'Alí on a teaching trip, He gave him some very specific teaching instructions. The whole passage is a key for success in teaching and I have used it for weekend seminars with excellent results.

Bahá'u'lláh

Instruction :

"A kindly approach and loving behavior toward the people are the first requirements of teaching the Cause. The teacher must carefully listen to whatever a person has to say—even hough his talk may consist only of vain imaginings and blind repetitions of the opinions of others. one should not resist or engage in argument. The teacher must avoid disputes which will end in stubborn refusal or hostility, because the other person will feel overpowered and defeated. Therefore he will be more inclined to reject the Cause. One should rather say, 'Maybe you are right but kindly consider the question from this other point of view.' Consideration, respect, and love, encourage people to listen and do not force them to respond with hostility. They are convinced because they see that your purpose is Not to defeat them, but to convey truth, to manifest courtesy, and to show forth heavenly attributes. This will encourage the people to be

fair. Their spiritual natures will respond, and by the bounty of God, they will find themselves recreated."

"Consider the way in which the Master teaches the people. He listens carefully to the most hollow and senseless talk, He listens so intently that the speaker says to himself, 'He is trying to learn from me.' Then the Master gradually and very carefully, by means that the other person does ot perceive, puts him on the right path and endows him with a fresh power of understanding."

DH 109-110

In regard to listening, the teacher must be genuinely interested. If you love someone, you are truly interested in everything that person has to say, no matter what they are talking about. Your mind is not occupied with the thoughts of what you are going to say until the one who is talking has finished. The teacher must learn not to interrupt or butt in while the person is talking. You must let them finish. Be polite, be courteous and be interested. You will note in the above quoted passage that Bahá'u'lláh uses the words **CAREFULLY LISTEN.** Now I can almost give you a guarantee that if you follow this instruction, the person you are trying to reach will lead you to the empty places in their heart that can be filled with the love of Bahá'u'lláh.

Bahá'u'lláh

Instruction :

"O My Friend, listen with heart and soul to the songs of the spirit, and treasure them as thine own eyes."

SV-37

During the mass teaching project in the Philippines, I went into a house and the woman said when I met her, "I am a Catholic, my mother is a Catholic and my daughter is a Catholic, and we will die Catholics." My response was, "That is wonderful, so few people really don't have anything anymore, why don't you tell me about your religion." This woman began to talk and as she spoke it became more and more obvious that she was very unhappy with the church. Things that had been weighing very heavy on her heart about God and religion came out one by one. Pent up emotions were finally released. I, for the most part, just carefully listened and responded with tender love and understanding and this woman, in two and a half hours, taught herself the Bahá'í Faith. The mother became a Bahá'í, the daughter became a Bahá'í and the grandmother became a Bahá'í.

Then we experienced an unexpected bonus. The grandfather had suffered a stroke, half of his body was paralyzed and he was confined to bed. This man, using his good arm and leg, rolled out of bed, pulled himself into the room where we had just finished the fireside and had enrolled his whole family. From the side of his mouth he said, "Alláh'u'Abhá." He had become a Bahá'í many years before. He was one of the first Bahá'ís in the country. When I left this woman said, "My father is a Bahá'í, my mother is a Bahá'í, my daughter is a Bahá'í and I am a Bahá'í. Thank God Bahá'u'lláh came. We will die Bahá'ís." This woman's daughter agreed to join the teaching team the next weekend, but came and told us that the day after we left her grandfather had peacefully passed away and she would have to stay home to help the family.

Universal House of Justice

Instruction :

> *"The unsophisticated people of the world
> . . .and they form the large majority of its
> population . . . have the same right to know of
> The Cause of God as others. When the
> friends are teaching the Word of God they
> should be careful to give the Message in the
> same simplicity as it is enunciated in our
> Teachings."*

LG-595

Another example from the Philippines: we went into a
house and the man, woman and children all came and sat
very respectfully. The teacher that was with me started to
speak. He never asked a single question nor did he have any
ideas where or what this precious humble family might want
to know. He just started to talk and he talked non-stop for
over two hours. He went from Siyyid Káẓim to the
Administrative order. After this long speech he asked them
if they had any questions and this sweet man looked
embarrassed, then smiled and said, "Do you like baseball?"
I later, sent some Philippino friends to visit and teach them.
They became Bahá'ís.

Bahá'u'lláh

Instruction :

> *"If ye be aware of a certain truth, if
> ye possess a jewel, of which others are
> deprived, share it with them in a language
> of utmost kindliness and good-will. If it
> be accepted, if it fulfil its purpose,
> your object is attained. If any one should*

*refuse it, leave him unto himself, and
beseech God to guide him."*

Gl-289

The teacher is also endowed with an extra sensory
perception, like all faculties, the more you use it the stronger
it becomes. This is called listening with your heart. For
example, a person may be saying, "I don't believe in God.
I hate religion. It is all a farce and why don't you just go
away and leave me alone?" What his heart may be saying
is, "Please prove to me I'm wrong."

Bahá'u'lláh

Instruction :

*"Say, implore God to open to your hearts
the portals of true understanding that ye
may be apprised of that which no one is
apprised."*

TB-188

The teacher must be very careful in these situations and
prayerfully judge them. The instructions from Bahá'u'lláh,
'Abdu'l-Bahá and the Guardian are very clear, if a person
is interested, then lovingly share with them the water of life,
if not, then we are commanded to leave them alone and pray
for them that God may graciously guide them.

CHAPTER 6

PRAYER AND INSPIRATION

Bahá'u'lláh

Instruction :

"O ye that dwell on earth! The religion of
God is for love and unity; make it not the
cause of enmity or dissension."

TB-220

We were doing the massive encounter in Alaska and were in the city of Ketchikan, doing street teaching. One team of five teachers met a man on the street and stopped to invite him to our evening meeting. When they asked him if he had heard of Bahá'u'lláh, he became furious and abusive, the Bahá'ís thought he was going to attack them. He became red in the face with anger and shouted, "I know your Bahá'u'lláh and I've read your Bahá'í books you ..." and he began to curse most abusively and screamed, "You anti-Christs!" The teachers apologized and politely excused themselves with, "We are sorry to have bothered and upset you. Please have a nice day." The teachers went off down the street with this man's curses ringing in their ears. They went around the corner and one of them said, "I think that is the kind of person that we must leave alone and pray for." So they all said a quick, "remover of difficulties," and went on with the teaching.

We had been maintaining a 24-hour prayer watch for over a year at this time, as the goal that Alaska had set for Massive Encounter was to reach and teach every single soul in Alaska. Or at least to let every soul know that Bahá'u'lláh has come, That He is a Messenger from God, and to give them the opportunity to accept or reject His message. So we stormed the very gates of heaven with prayer. With the large teams, we would have 3 to 10 teachers on prayer watch at a time. These friends would pray from say 3 AM to 4 AM and then the next group would relieve them and they would go back to bed. Even during the day we would have a few Bahá'ís stay in and back up the teachers with prayers. This also gave the team members a break from the daily grind of teaching and reinvigorated them for the work. I am sure that in many countries where we were able to initiate the prayer watch it was one of the major keys to our successful teaching.

These 5 teachers that had met the angry man, each had been put on theprayer watch. One had prayers from 1 AM to 2 AM, the next from 2 AM to 3 AM, thus following each other right up to 6 AM. These precious hearts, without consulting each other, told me later that they could not get that angry man from the morning out of their minds, and each of them, on their own, decided to spend their hour of prayer praying for the angry man. Most teachers make the mistake of reading an instruction and then just follow part of it, like, "leave them alone," and neglect the part about, "pray for them, that God may graciously guide them."

That very night when the people were coming for our meeting, one of these teachers rushed up to me and told me that the angry man from the previous day was entering the Bahá'í meeting hall. I intercepted him and told him that we were very sorry for invading his privacy and upsetting him on the street. This man was very polite and said he had come over to apologize for his actions on the street yesterday. I told him that was not necessary but he insisted, stating that last night he had lain awake all night, could not sleep and that he knew if he did not come over and apologize for his bad behavior, he would never sleep again. I accepted his apology and invited him in for the program.

He then asked me if I knew who the anti-Christ was and he went on to explain that he was the anti-Christ. Yesterday on the street the Bahá'ís were Christ-like. I was cursing and swearing and wanting to kill and I was surely not like Christ "Yes,"he said, "I am the anti-Christ. Another thing, as I lay awake I came to the conclusion that my minister was wrong, Bahá'u'lláh was true, and I want to be a Bahá'í."

Bahá'u'lláh

Instruction :

"Proclaim, then, that which the Most Great Spirit will inspire thee to utter in the service of the Cause of thy Lord, that thou mayest stir up the souls of all men and incline their hearts unto this most blessed and all-glorious Court."

Gl-303

Another example of listening with the spiritual ears of the heart took place during a mass teaching effort in Nigeria. We were about 300 miles back in the bush out of Lagos. This was a first attempt by the pioneers and local African Bahá'ís at mass teaching, as my visit was a very short one, I longed to really help them get off to a good start. Upon our arrival in this village we went to the headman to pay our respects and to get his permission for a meeting. This man, in fact, was more like a king than a headman. He had gone to Oxford University in England and so of course he spoke a very beautiful English with a strong British accent. He not only gave us permission for the meeting but offered his services as a translator into the native bush dialect.

When we left his house I started down a trail. My Bahá'í translator stopped me, and told me I was going the long way to the center of the village, he further explained that he had grown up in this village so he knew it well. I asked him if we could get to the center of the village where the meeting was to be held if we went this way. He laughed good naturedly and said, "Yes." As we proceeded along the trail, three very tall and ebony black women with very bright colored dresses, were coming down the trail leaving the village. They were indeed very beautiful, with bright and shining faces. I asked my translator to invite these black jewels of light to come to our meeting. All three turned around and accompanied us to the meeting place.

There were about 1500 people present. They were all sitting on the floor of the central plaza and the oil lamps were lit around the perimeter of the plaza. When I looked out at my audience, all I could see were the whites of their eyes, because the lamps were up high and they were sitting on the floor. I gave a very short introductory talk which the headman translated, and every time I stopped for translation, I repeated over and over in my heart the Greatest Name. The reason for doing this is because it is one of the instructions.

Bahá'u'lláh

Instruction :

> *"Whoso openeth his lips in this day, and maketh mention of the name of his Lord, the hosts of Divine inspiration shall descend upon him. On him shall also descend the Concourse on High, each bearing aloft a chalice of pure light."*

ADJ-71

Bahá'u'lláh said it. The conditions of receiving these bounties are to make mention the name of our Lord. Who is our Lord? Bahá'u'lláh of course. Not only can the teacher do this in their heart but can also do it openly. For example, while teaching, the teacher can say Bahá'u'lláh said this and Bahá'u'lláh said that or Bahá'u'lláh taught this and Bahá'u'lláh taught that.

After the short introductory talk I opened it for questions. We have learned, again through the school of much experience, that having questions from the floor is not the best way. The best way is that after the talk is finished, tell your audience that anyone who has questions can ask them of any of the Bahá'ís present, using Bahá'í buttons or another way of identifying the Bahá'ís.

What often happens when you are most successful in your day to day mass teaching and are enrolling large numbers of Bahá'ís, is that the opposition can become well organized. They will use your Bahá'í meetings during the question periods to take over. In the guise of seekers, they will try to plant doubts and confusion in the minds of the people and try to turn them away from the truth. Very successful mass teaching always comes down in the end to one on one firesides anyway. The sooner the Bahá'ís can get heart to heart with the individuals the better. I have had these trouble makers still try to take over. When I tell them if they have any questions, to ask the other Bahá'ís, they will say that they are sure everyone present is interested in their questions. To which I reply, "Would everyone interested in this gentleman's questions please go over in the corner and a Bahá'í will be there to answer them." Each time this has happened the only people over in the corner are the people that have come together from the opposition to disrupt our meeting. Again I would like to restate the position to never cast anything in concrete, to be flexible and to change to meet the occasion. The reason for asking for questions in

Nigeria was because I only had one Bahá'í translator on the team that spoke the native dialect.

Each time a question was being asked in the Nigerians native dialect, I repeated in my heart the Greatest Name and then, when it was repeated in English, the knowledge flooded into my heart and mind, not just the obvious question, but the reason behind the question. It was about 11 PM when one of the people stood up into the light where he was sure everyone could see who he was and he turned several times, 360 degree circles, to insure that everyone would recognize him. Then he said in a strong emotional voice, "With the answer to that last question, for the first time in my life, I am at peace with the knowledge of God and I am convinced that my Muslim and Juju brothers' worship that same God that I do."(The village was made up of three distinct groups, Muslims, Christians and Jujus.)

One after another nine people stood up and made their dramatic declarations in the same way. We then retired to the king's house where we were lovingly invited to spend the night. I then sat with this man, who was a very devout and sincere Christian, and listened to him and loved him and I shared with him the water of life. He was a physically huge man and at about 2 AM, he smashed his fist onto the table and shouted, "If I turn my back on Bahá'u'lláh I will have to turn my back on my Lord and Savior Jesus Christ. I can't do that! I can't do that! I can't do that!" So he made the tenth Bahá'í in that village.

The next morning at dawn, one of those beautiful black jewels that we had gone down the wrong trail to intercept knocked at our door. If she was radiantly beautiful the day before, you should have seen her that morning. She was so radiant, and she declared that she had stayed up praying all night that if Bahá'u'lláh was true that she would be allowed by God to recognize Him. At first light this morning she had been confirmed and she stated that she wanted to be a Bahá'í, and she was sure her whole family also wanted to be Bahá'ís. So we left the remote village with a strong community of 11 new additions to our Bahá'í family.

It is difficult to explain the spiritual principle involved in this concept of listening with your heart, as it is an intangible.

CHAPTER 7

FOLLOW YOUR HEART

Bahá'u'lláh

Instruction :

"O My friend, listen with heart and soul to the songs of the spirit, and treasure them as thine own eyes."

SV-37

We were on a mass teaching effort in the Yukon Territory of Canada in a village called Upper Laiard. It was an Indian village, and in the meeting was one drunk who was loud, abusive and vulgar. So the other Indians in the meeting took this guy and threw him out and locked the door. We had finished the meeting and I had just invited all the people to form a big unity circle. We were all holding hands and were singing Alláh-u-Abhá (which I had explained and taught them), when the door flew open and this drunken Indian had broken it open, came into the room with murder in his eyes. Yet somehow I heard the cry of his heart and it said, "I'm a human being too and you can't treat me this way and I am going to kill everyone in here." So I intercepted him and took him into my arms and whispered into his ear, "Yes, you are a wonderful human being and we love you very much. You are very precious to us." He stepped back and the murder went out of his eyes and he turned around and left the hall.

Another example of this took place in Prince Rupert, in Canada. One of our mass teachers, a Tlingit Indian woman, told me that she stopped at a house during a door

to door invitational effort and that a woman came to the
door and was very angry and said, "Go away. Leave me
alone." and slammed the door in the teacher's face. This
teacher said that she did not feel right about this. She knew
that Bahá'u'lláh had said to leave them alone if they were
not interested, but she had a very strong desire to go back
again.

She asked me what she should do. I told her to follow
her heart, as Bahá'u'lláh said he would inspire the heart,
he never said he would inspire the mind. So she returned
to the house the next day. The lady opened the door and
her first words were, "Thank God you have come back.
I was praying that you would return." She then went on
to explain that when this teacher had come before, the
baby had messed all over its crib, the washing machine
had just broken and the water was running all over the
floor and the phone was ringing. She was very sorry she
had been so rude. They had a wonderful fireside and this
precious heart became a Bahá'í.

A book could probably be filled with all the times
we have seen the miraculous results of this following the
heart, or listening with your heart. Many times when a
teacher has had an overpowering desire to go to a certain
place, or stop and talk to someone, and sometimes it seems
to defy reason.

One such time was when I was pioneering in Mexico.
It was in the state of Oaxaca, and the goal of the nine-
year plan was to have at least one Bahá'í in each state
of Mexico. By just living in Oaxaca the goal was met.
We had been there about 2 years and through the mass
teaching effort had opened up about 95 villages. My goal
was to open and consolidate nine villages. That was my
plan, not Bahá'u'lláh's plan. In truth what would happen
is; I would be going to a newly opened village and upon

my arrival some new Bahá'ís would be found who did not live in that village, but were there visiting. Then in trying to follow the instructions as to lovingly deepen these new Bahá'ís and not leave them to their own devices, I would be obligated to go visit them.

As you can well imagine, I was going from village to village from sun up to late at night day after day, month after month and year after year non-stop. Still the work piled up. So it was against all reason and made no sense at all to try to open another village, yet one morning I advised another teacher that was with me, "Today we are going to Taviche."

"Where is Taviche?" this teacher asked.

"I don't know, I've never heard of it," I replied.

We checked the map, sure enough, there was a village named Taviche. It was at the end of a small narrow gage train track. We were delighted to be able to ride on a train for a change instead of driving or hiking, which was the norm. On the train into Taviche we tried unsuccessfully to talk to the people. When the train finally arrived at the end of the line there was only a train station and no village. I asked the train conductor where Taviche was and he said it was about half a kilometer up the trail. I explained that we wanted to go to Taviche and he said, "Go ahead."

"But," I replied, "I also want to go back to the city on the train."

The conductor laughed and said, "Well, I'm sorry but you can't do both. The train turns around here and in 10 minutes will return to the city." He further explained that there was no place to stay in the village, and that the only way out, other than by train, was to hike across the desert to the highway and catch the bus. This trek was over 10 miles.

Reason and common sense now took hold and in my mind I wrote off Taviche, and went off to play with some children that had come to meet the train. The other Bahá'í teacher stayed and talked to this conductor, with the hope of a fireside with him. Later on in the train my companion said, "Do you know what that conductor said to me? He told me no one in the whole world cares anything about the people that live in Taviche."

This remark went right to my heart, and I declared that on the following day we would return to Taviche, with proper big sombreros or hats and plenty of water, we would tell the people that there were people all over the world that loved them and cared about them. Then we would make our trek to the highway across the desert.

The next morning, with my sons to help carry the lunch and water andwith the other Bahá'í teacher, we were on the train once again for Taviche. We waved good-by to the conductor and set off up the trail to Taviche. The feeling I had was that someone was pulling me up that trail. When we rounded a bend in the trail, Taviche came into view and it was on the side of a hill. My friend said, "Let's go up the hill and visit the houses and work our way down and out of the village."

"No," I said.

"OK," she replied. "Let's start up the hill and visit all the houses and then come down and out of the village."

"No," I again answered her. "We are going to that house right up there." Which we proceeded to do. When we knocked on the door a beautiful young man opened the door and lovingly invited us in and told us to sit down.

"Why have you come here," he said.

"For God," I replied.

"Listen to me," he interrupted. "I'm going to tell you why you have come. Last night in my dream, you two foreigners came to me and told me that you were coming to bring me a new message from God. I stayed home and cleaned my house and waited for you to come." Now, although the Bahá'í teacher with me came from Venezuela, she was dark skinned, with black hair, black eyes and looked like any other Mexican. Up to this time she had not said a single word, yet this man used the word foreigners. His name was Efraen Hernandez de Perez. He had graduated from the University and had returned to that village because he wanted to help his people. I am reminded of the statement of Bahá'u'lláh that if a jewel lies hidden beyond the seven seas and under a mountain that He has been empowered to expose it and bring it to light.

Bahá'u'lláh

Instruction :

> *"If one speck of a jewel be lost and buried beneath a mountain of stones, and lie hidden beyond the seven seas, the Hand of Omnipotence would assuredly reveal it in this Day, pure and cleansed from dross."*

ADJ-67

This man most enthusiastically accepted the Cause and wanted something to read. Because we knew we would have to hike through the desert we had tried to keep our load down, so had not brought any books with us. We then proceeded up the mountain, and never had we been met with such animosity. When we tried to speak to the people they would actually spit and turn away. The other teacher offered a woman a pamphlet and this woman snatched the tract out of the teacher's hand, tore it up and threw it on the ground.

We returned to Efraen and explained that we had so many villages, and so many Bahá'ís that were eager and hungry for the heavenly table, that we felt compelled to leave Taviche. This precious soul pleaded that at least we must bring him some books, which we promised to do but set no time. We then hiked out through the desert to the highway and back to the city.

It was about six months later after I had bought a 4-wheel drive, all terrain vehicle, that I drove across the desert to see Efraen in Taviche. He was not at home, so we left the books and promised to return the first Sunday two months away. We asked his wife to tell him to expect us, barring some unforeseen problem, we would surely come.

The story of this young man spread across Mexico and several Bahá'ís, including the Continental Councillor in Mexico at that time, accompanied us on this planned visit to meet such an outstanding Bahá'í. As planned, we arrived in Taviche and when we inquired for Efraen were advised that he was dead. I was amazed and said, "But he is a young man and two months ago was out working in his field when we came."

"He's dead," was the reply. "The whole family is putting the marker on his grave today."

Bahá'u'lláh

Instruction :

"O SON OF THE SUPREME!
I have made death a messenger of joy
to thee Wherefore dost thou grieve."

HWA #32

We went to Efraen's mother's house and there were around 15 adults and a number of children were present. The sadness was over powering and we all went to work to help ease this grieving family through their ordeal. I talked to the mother, held her hand and explained about life after death and God, like a loving gardener transplanting her son from a dark and gloomy world into a world of light. The grief was still there but it was no longer as oppressive and the mother said, "I want to tell you all how my son died." So I called over the Councillor and the other Bahá'ís all gathered around. The Councillor was a native of Mexico and a native speaker so there can be no doubt about this story.

"I heard that my son was sick," she said. "So I went to see him. He had a slight fever. He told me that he tried to tell the people of Taviche about Bahá'í but no one would listen. So he decided that he would give his life so that the people of Taviche would learn and accept the Cause of God. I cried out, 'No! No! let me go get the priest.' My son looked at me very sternly and said, "Mother, mother please don't take me away from my God." In three days this young man was dead. We then went with the family to the grave site for prayers. Because we were on the edge of the desert the weather was extremely hot, but the Councillor, who was wearing a sleeveless blouse, had goose bumps on her arms from the special spiritual atmosphere at that grave-side. We then went back to the mother's house where Efraen's wife was waiting for us with the Bahá'í books we had left two months before. On the fly-leaf of each well-used book Efraen had written, "Praise be to God, the Lord of Eternity." He had signed his name and dated the books. That day the whole family became Bahá'ís, so we had 15 wonderful new friends in Taviche. Within 6 months the whole village was transformed and when I would drive into the village, the people would hear my truck and rush out and plead with me to come to their house that day and talk about God with them.

CHAPTER 8

FOUNDATION OF ALL HUMAN VIRTUES

I would like to digress for a moment and dispel once and for all the nonsense about food and eating with the natives. That is the myth that people will be offended if you refuse their food. Believe me they are far more offended when you vomit in your plate trying to eat something you don't like. I have been with Eskimos in the Arctic, the remotest jungles where the Indians still shoot monkeys out of the trees with blow guns, and in the most cosmopolitan cities on the planet earth, and I have discovered that even some members of the same family have their likes and dislikes about some foods. No one I have ever met has felt the least bit offended when I or any of the Bahá'ís with me said they did not like something. As a matter of fact sometimes I have been tested by practical jokers that try to feed me something that they would never eat themselves. So I have the policy, I will eat it only if the natives eat it. Not once, but many times, we have had the experience of training mass teachers and telling them very carefully that if someone serves them something that is repugnant to them, just push it aside and leave it and don't make a big show of your dislike. Yet time and again, even after this consultation, when a person is served black beetle soup in the back country of Thailand, he or she comes out with a soul stirring, "YUCK!" and an expression of horror on their faces and this does indeed insult the people.

You understand that I loved Efraen's mother very much, and on my first return visit to the village this wonderful woman told me that she had cooked, especially for me, her favorite soup. It was truly awful for me. Now, instead of being truthful with her and telling her that the soup was different and too rich for my foreign stomach, I forced myself to eat it, then got in my truck, drove out of the village, stopped my truck behind a big rock and up came the soup. Of course the next month and the next and the next for about six months I had a monthly stomach cleaning at the big rock. For, because of my not being truthful about the soup, she thought I really liked it so she fixed it for me every month. Finally because we loved each other very much I got up my courage and told her that her wonderful soup did not agree with my stomach. She understood completely and gave me a coke instead, but by now I had been so conditioned psychologically that I stopped at the big rock and up came the coke. This comes back to the principle, "FOLLOW THE INSTRUCTIONS."

'Abdu'l-Bahá

Instruction :

> *"Truthfulness is the foundation of all human virtues. Without truthfulness progress and success, in all the worlds of God, are impossible for any soul. When this holy attribute is established in man, all the divine qualities will also be acquired."*

ADJ-22

Bahá'u'lláh is very clear on truthfulness and honesty. Yet we listen to every Tom, Dick and Harry who think they know better than Bahá'u'lláh. We are either untruthful by words or by actions, and then we must suffer the consequences.

CHAPTER 9

TENDER LOVING CARE (TLC)

'Abdu'l-Bahá

Instruction :

"Be a sign of love, a manifestation of mercy, a fountain of tenderness, kind-hearted, good to all and gentle to the servants of God."

TAB-620

The teacher must reach out and show the real spirit of love to each and every person that Bahá'u'lláh puts them into contact with. My experience in Mexico taught me this in a very dramatic way. We found, after about 2 years, we had enrolled so many new believers, I could not remember who was Bahá'í and who was not, so every person I met coming and going to the villages I treated like the dearest Bahá'í friend. The following letter, written to the National Spiritual Assembly of Taiwan, is self explanatory and helps make this point.

July 17, 1989

"Dear Bahá'í Friends,

On the week-end of the 8th and 9th of July I was invited to go to Taichung and conduct a week-end deepening with the new Bahá'ís. I took a new Bahá'í from Hsinchu as my translator and this was her first Bahá'í meeting outside of Hsinchu. The atmosphere was wonderful, the Bahá'í teachers were warm and friendly and the new Bahá'ís were great. They were very sincere, open hearted and eager to learn. Our new Bahá'í, was very impressed and was delighted that she was a Bahá'í and belonged to such a wonderful family and now she wants to take her non-Bahá'í husband to some other meetings in the future. The changes that I experienced with the team since the last number of times that I went out were most encouraging and a step in the right direction. Also the caliber of the newly enrolled Bahá'ís shows that the NSA's plans and efforts are very fruitful.

The 13th of July there was another new enrollment in Hsinchu and he has been reading and studying the Faith for about a year. He has become enchanted with the Hidden Words and has been using the Bahá'í prayers daily. When he told me that he was changing jobs I asked him if he would like to join the teaching team as long as he was free and he was most enthusiastic and agreed to go for at least a week. He is a local Chinese and does not speak any English. I told him he would stay with the team and the arrangements would be made for him. Because I had been so impressed with the team and the new believers in Taichung, I felt that the party scheduled for the 15th at a Bahá'í's house with the team would be a loving entrance for this brand new Bahá'í to meet his team mates.

I called the National Spiritual Assembly office to talk to the team coordinator when it opened on Friday morning. She was on the phone so I explained to the girl who answered about the new Bahá'í and asked that she call me back as soon as she was off of the phone. I waited all day for the call back and late in the afternoon I called again and told her about the new Bahá'í from Hsinchu. The team coordinator had not received my message. As I was already booked up solid for the week-end, I asked a Bahá'í who has been a Bahá'í for over a year and since has been some what inactive if she would take this man to Taichung. She agreed. I was elated because I felt that if she could also experience that true spirit of Bahá'í love and unity that we felt the previous week-end she might be caught up again in the spirit of the faith. I then called the Bahá'í center in Taichung and spoke to the Englishman and told him about them and asked him to pass on the information to the teaching team and to make a special effort of tender loving care (TLC) of these two precious souls. I also called the Auxiliary Board Member but he said he would not be at the party, but I asked him to contact the team and encourage them to make sure these two got some real Bahá'í treatment. He assured me that he would.

They were asked to go directly to the home in Taichung and the team would look after them upon arrival. Later I learned that they were back in Hsinchu. They were made to feel like outsiders and not welcome. One Chinese from Malaysia spoke to them and said he knew that the man was to join the team and go with them to Taipei but he would have to get his own bus ticket as he did not have a ticket for him. Then he asked him where he planned to stay and said he would have to stay in a hotel. He then left and never spoke to them again. The Iranian lady from Oman was friendly and loving and one boy from Canada talked to them for a few minutes.

They stayed in the corner and felt embarrassed and finally escaped and came back home.

Now this problem is due entirely to inadequate training of the teachers. I have encountered this problem the first time in Mexico during mass teaching in 1964 and later during mass teaching in South Carolina. First the Bahá'í teachers grow to love each other so much and they feel very comfortable and safe with each other and all new members would be made to feel a little like outsiders. Second, the attitude develops of we the teachers and they the other Bahá'ís. The third problem is, we the Bahá'ís and they the non-Bahá'ís. You MUST educate the teachers and re-enforce it through your daily consultations that there is no we and they. It is just us, all humanity and each soul that Bahá'u'lláh puts us into contact with is unique and wonderful and put forth all our effort to show that human soul that we love them and our love is true and spiritual. This works in strengthening the team members in their relationships on the team as well as with non-Bahá'í or new Bahá'í contacts and with the entire Bahá'í family. We as followers of the Blessed Beauty must strive with heart and soul to make every soul feel that Divine Spirit of His Cause and share in that unique spirit of love that can only be generated by His Spirit." The end of the letter.

CHAPTER 10

DIVINE EDUCATION

Bahá'u'lláh

Instruction :

*"That one indeed is a man who, today,
dedicateth himself to the service of the entire
human race. . . . It is not for him to pride
himself who loveth his own country, but
rather for him who loveth the whole world.
The earth is but one country, and mankind
its citizens."*

Gl-250

I am convinced, however, as already stated, that
Bahá'u'lláh is the Supreme Commander and He is directing
this dramatic engagement from His retreats of Glory. There
is the fact that nothing can befall the lovers of Bahá'u'lláh
except what He has ordained for their sake or the sake
of those around them. In the above incident about this
new Bahá'í, we can see that this kind of thing happens
as part of our divine education. So we can't say it was
a mistake.

Bahá'u'lláh

Instruction :

*"Nothing can befall us but what God hath
destined for us."*

SV-35

Another story that will help illustrate this point follows: I was coming down the trail out of Zoquiapan, in Oaxaca, Mexico when I met a beautiful young man on the trail on his way in. The conversation went something like this;

"What are you doing way back here?" he asked.

"I am telling everyone about the wonderful news that Christ has returned," I replied.

"That's wonderful, that's wonderful, I have been expecting Him. What is his new name? The Bible says he will come with a new name."

"Bahá'u'lláh, which means the Glory of God," I explained.

This young man was so delighted and excited with my answers that he could hardly contain himself as he enthused, "He said He would return in the Glory of His Father and He did, He did it."

Because it was getting late and I was in a hurry, which one must never be when teaching the Cause, I asked this man if He believed what I said and understood and when he assured me that he did I gave him the enrollment card and he unhesitatingly signed it. I was putting the card in my pocket and giving him a prayer book when he said, "Now we must tell everyone the good news and have all our meetings on Saturday."

"Wait a minute," I said. Not understanding what he was talking about. "Saturday? why Saturday?"

"Because the Bible said so, that's why. Another thing these pictures of Saints and altars people have in their houses must be thrown out. I've got to go." And he prepared to depart.

"Wait a minute, just a minute." I shouted, as it dawned on me that this man was a confirmed Seventh Day Adventist, I learned later that he had been trained in the U.S., they had taught him to expect the return of Christ like a thief in the night and all the signs of His expected return.

"No, I don't have time, I am already late." With that he took off up the mountain.

I sat on a rock at the side of the trail and I wanted to cry. What had I done? I thought. I had visions of Cristiano (that was his name) going through the mountains telling everyone that Bahá'ís believed in Saturday and they had to get rid of all their family heir looms. These so-called altars people have in their homes are passed on from daughter to daughter and each generation adds to them and they justifiably are the most valued possessions people have. They are an anchor to the past and a connection with God for the present and something to leave to their children for the future. So I determined that I would hold Cristiano's card and the next month when I came to visit, I would set him straight even if it meant tearing up his card.

Well, the next month and each month thereafter when I was in the Village, Cristiano was out and when I was out, he was in. At this time we had Bahá'ís all over the mountains and so I enquired about Cristiano. I was advised by everyone that he was a most wonderful Bahá'í and he was holding classes and teaching everyone about Bahá'í. I wondered what on earth he could be teaching as the only book I had given him was a prayer book. I also asked when he had his meetings and was informed that he had them every Saturday. The following Riḍván, Cristiano was elected delegate to the National Spiritual Assembly Convention from that area and I was all set to confront this guy on Saturday and the Saints at the convention. Well, he never made it.

It was almost a year to the day, I was going into Zoquiapan on my monthly schedule of consolidation and teaching and a very beautiful young man walks up along side of me and says, "Do you remember me, I'm Cristiano."

I was, of course, delighted for my longed for confrontation could now take place, as we both were going into the village and as it was about a 15-mile hike, I felt I had plenty of time to set this Saturday and Saint guy straight.

Cristiano was full of questions and needed answers for his Bahá'í classes. His questions were deep and thoughtful questions, and ranged from marriage, divorce, birth, death and to the Administrative order. He was eager and excited and not once did he question the answers that differed from the Bible. He seemed to completely accept the authority of Bahá'u'lláh. Then as we hiked along up and down the mountains, Cristiano said, "This Bahá'í religion is not just for Saturday you know, it is for every minute, hour and day of your entire life." So he just wiped out in one sentence my year of anxiety over Saturday.

A few miles later as we stopped on the trail to rest this wonderful Bahá'í teacher asked me if I knew who the Saints were and I answered with a question, "Please tell me what you think, who are they?"

"Well," he explained, "They are people just like you and me, except that they do exactly what God says to do and they don't ever do what He says not to do. So they are saints and if the people want to have their pictures and things in their homes to remind them of these wonderful people, what harm is there in this?"

Thank God that He protected this rare jewel of a Bahá'í from the ignorance of Jenabe. I then told Cristiano about my favorite Saint.

'Abdu'l-Bahá

Instruction :

"Saints are men who have freed themselves from the world of matter and who have overcome sin. They live in the world but are not of it, their thoughts being continually in the world of the spirit. Their lives are spent in holiness, and their deeds show forth love, justice and godliness. They are illumined from on high; they are as bright and shining lamps in the dark places of the earth. These are the saints of God."

PT 60-61

A long time ago in the land called Spain there was a small black child, his name was Martin and he was an orphan. He went to the church and he felt that these men of God would be his mother and father. What happened, of course, was that little Martin became a slave to every novitiate studying to become a priest. It was, "Martin do this. Martin do that. Martin bring me this. Martin bring me that." This little child worked from dawn to late at night, sure in his little heart that by serving these men of God, he was indeed serving God. Then one day the Bishop came to visit and little Martin was sure that the Bishop was indeed and in fact the incarnation of Saint Peter himself. So when the Bishop entered the church and some rats ran across the floor and he turned to little Martin and shouted, "You there, get rid of these rats in the Church." Martin was thunderstruck.

That night after he finished his work for the day little Martin went into the church and prostrated himself under the altar and wept. He prayed, "O Jesus! You know Martin can't even catch one rat and there are hundreds maybe even thousands of rats in the church. Please, please, you help

Martin as I only want to do what you want me to do." So
he wept and prayed all night. So the story goes, all the rats
left the church that night. From that day to this no rats have
ever come back into that church. True or not, it is the kind
of story and he was the kind of a pure hearted child, that
warms my heart and inspires me to greater service. So my
favorite saint is, Saint Martin.

CHAPTER 11

PICK AND CHOOSE

Bahá'u'lláh

Instruction :

*"Wholly for the sake of God he should
proclaim His message, and with that same
spirit accept whatever response his words
may evoke in his hearer."*

Gl-339

This problem of choosing and picking the new Bahá'ís
is a problem that most teachers consciously or subconsciously
do. We think this one or that one would make a wonderful
Bahá'í and this one or that one could never make it. The
truth is that the statement of Jesus, "That many are called
and few are chosen," has a double meaning. First is that
God does the picking and choosing, the 2nd is that the
person being taught does the choosing to be a Bahá'í or
not. The truth is that the teacher is only the channel through
which the grace of God flows to humanity and is certainly
not the judge. The incident with Cristiano is a good example
of this.

The goal of the nine-year plan was to have 10 Local
Spiritual Assemblies in the Yukon territory of Canada and
at the point of starting a mass teaching campaign we only
had one. Our team was 15 wonderful souls from Alaska and
a few wonderful local Bahá'ís from Whitehorse.

The first village we went into was named Carmaks and
was an Indian village. For most of the teachers this was the

first time in a mass teaching project and, one and all, they came to me one by one and complained about an Indian, over by the door, signing a Bahá'í card who was so drunk that they claimed he didn't know what he was doing and should not be allowed to do that. I explained that what the man was holding was only a piece of cardboard and that in a few days the follow up team would be coming through. If the man did not know what he was doing that small piece of cardboard could be torn up.

Bahá'u'lláh

Instruction:

O   YE   RICH   ONES   ON   EARTH!
The poor in your midst are My trust; guard
ye   My   trust."

HWP-#54

I also tried to tell the teachers that this statement of Bahá'u'lláh's was for just these kind of people. Who else could be so poor. Unloved, in fact hated, their culture destroyed, forced to live in squalor and poverty with no future. One of the means the invaders used to subdue this formerly proud people was to get them addicted to alcohol. So I advised them one and all to show everyone the true spirit of Bahá'í love and to be especially tender and loving to these dispirited people. Some of the teachers went on to complain that if this was mass teaching of drunks they didn't want to be mass teachers.

Nineteen days later we had formed eleven Local Assemblies and were holding a wonderful victory conference in Whitehorse. Hand of the Cause Enoch Olinga, the father of victories, came to lead the celebration. We were in the hall and the setting was indeed very beautiful. The table was covered with a white table cloth and in the center was a large bouquet of red roses. The chairman was a blond woman, who was dressed to kill, and behind the table sat beautiful black Hand of the Cause Enoch Olinga with that wonderful enigmatic smile of love that seemed to radiate from him. In walked this Indian from Carmaks and he walked right up to the front of the room, sober and head held high.

This now completed the picture of red, white and black. One could tell that the Indian was a little nervous as he looked at Enoch and felt the perpetual love that emanated from him, thus encouraged by it, he said in a loud and ringing voice. "I come from Carmaks and I lost my heart. I didn't have a heart and the Bahá'ís came to my village and they gave me back my heart, they gave me back my heart. Thank you- thank you," and he went and sat down. Now for the sake of a little piece of cardboard we could have missed giving this man back his heart.

'Abdu'l-Bahá

Instruction :

> *"'For many are called, but few are chosen.' That is, to many is it offered, but rare is the soul who is singled out to receive the great bestowal of guidance. 'Such is the bounty of God: to whom He will He giveth it, and of immense bounty is God.'"*

SAB-9

However, and I must state this, it is not our custom, or do we seek out drunks to teach and I instruct the teachers to avoid these places while teaching. If we have the certitude that Bahá'u'lláh is in fact the Supreme Commander and He is indeed directing this dramatic engagement from His retreats of Glory, we can accept the exceptions.

I was with the mass teaching team in Guyana and had just given the above instructions to the team about avoiding the bars and was walking down the street. A group of men were standing outside the bar waiting for it to open and as I passed, they in good humor, called me over more for fun than serious. I did not want to stop but they were insistent so I went over. They began to ask questions and in no time the gathering had turned serious. One of the questions they asked was about drinking alcohol. I very carefully explained the law as a law of love from a loving Creator. Then one of the men said, "Mister, I want to be a Bahá'í." His friends all laughed and asked him if he didn't understand what I had just said, that Bahá'ís don't drink and he was the biggest drunk in town. So I ignored his request and went on answering questions. In a few minutes I felt a tug on my arm and turned around and here was the same man. He looked me right in the eye and said, "Mister, in my heart of hearts I want to be a Bahá'í." I reached into my pocket and gave him the enrollment card forthwith without a question.

Bahá'u'lláh

Instruction:

> *"Beware lest ye exchange the Wine of God for your own wine, for it will stupefy your minds, and turn your faces away from the Countenance of God, the All-Glorious, the Peerless, the Inaccessible. Approach it not, for it hath been forbidden unto you by the behest of God, The Exalted, the Almighty."*

KA-n145

CHAPTER 12

OBEY THE LAWS

Before I leave the drunks and the problem of alcohol it is a law of God that we do not drink and the law is clear and explicit. The Bahá'í teachers must never tell the student or seeker that it is OK or in any way water down the laws of God. This is one of the big problems that has led to the decline of religions throughout the world. Man wants to change the laws of God to suit man and it is man that must change to obey the laws of God. We as teachers must learn to give the laws in a tender and loving way but give them we must.

Shoghi Effendi

Instruction :

"Let him refrain, at the outset, from insisting on such laws and observances as might impose to severe a strain on the seeker's newly-awakened faith, and endeavor to nurse him, patiently, tactfully, and determinedly, into full maturity,"

ADJ-43

The Guardian said on the acceptance of new believers not to make it hard or difficult for them but he also said that in the process of enrolling they must be informed of the laws they must follow.

Universal House of Justice

Instruction :

"The declarants need not know all the proofs, history, laws, and principles of the

Faith, but in the process of declaring themselves they must, in addition to catching the spark of faith become basically informed about the Central Figures of the Faith, as well as the existence of laws they must follow and administration they must obey."

WG-32

CHAPTER 13

LIVE THE LIFE AND SERVE

The Cause of God has the mystic power to change the human being into a new creation and this is done through our obedience to the laws and in no other way. The best mass teacher or individual teacher is that great silent teacher of "my inner life and private character." in other words the extent to which I obey the laws in both letter and spirit and thus lead an exemplary Bahá'í life. Not only is trying to live a Bahá'í life the best teacher but, in fact, is the most wonderful means of consolidation after the soul has accepted Bahá'u'lláh.

Shoghi Effendi

Instruction :

"Not by the force of numbers, not by the mere exposition of a set of new and noble principles, not by an organized campaign of teaching—no matter how worldwide and elaborate in its character—not even by the staunchness of our faith or the exaltation of our enthusiasm, can we ultimately hope to vindicate in the eyes of a critical and skeptical age the supreme claim of the Abhá Revelation. One thing and only one thing will unfailingly and alone secure the undoubted triumph of this sacred Cause, namely, the extent to whichour own inner life and private character mirror forth in their manifold aspects the splendor ofthose eternalprinciples proclaimed by Bahá'u'lláh."

We were doing Massive Encounter in Alaska and we had a core group of between 15 and 30 full time teachers from the beginning to the end. This campaign lasted for over three years. One of the Bahá'ís on the team had left his home, and his town was a goal town. He was quite wealthy and had purchased a beautiful home on a hill overlooking the town. Almost every day this dedicated soul would lament and complain about his failure as a pioneer, as not one single soul was even interested in the Faith. He had left his beautiful wife and wonderful children and stayed on the Alaskan teaching team for the full campaign.

At the end of the first year, when we had gone to Southeastern Alaska for the winter and were not too far away from this dedicated teacher's goal town, I requested permission to take the team over there, and try to help this precious family win their goals. The National Spiritual Assembly of Alaska gave us permission to go in for a week-end.

We hit the streets of that town and, as the weather was below freezing, we went from house to house and invited everyone to a public meeting. As usual when we extended this loving invitation, if the person was interested, we stopped and gave them the message. As it was in the middle of winter and nothing else was going on in the town, almost everyone came. As the people came in we gave them a pencil and an enrollment card.

After the music and the talk we invited the whole town to fill in the cards and that night we collected 19 signed cards. I must digress for a moment from this theme and point out that this type of teaching is not mass teaching and it is not even mass reaching. It is mass card collecting and not heart collecting. Real mass teaching always comes down to one to one, eye to eye, knee to knee and heart to heart. The seeker has an individual fireside where all of his questions are most carefully explained and the heart is deeply touched by the beauty of the Faith. We have learollecting and do not really try to teach, that a great deal of time, money and energy are dissipated and lost in trying to sort out the mess. A mess it usually is.

Now back to my story. That night I gave all 19 signed cards to my team mate's wife and the next morning the team left and her husband left with us. About a week later I received a phone call from the elegant lady and she said, "Jenabe what do I do with these cards?"

I said, "Well, why don't you try going to visit them."

It was about six weeks later when I got another phone call. This woman was in tears and she explained, "I went to visit all 19 of them and it was awful. The weather was freezing and no one even invited me in. In fact, most of them were rude and even shut the door in my face. Oh Jenabe, what can I do?"

" Why don't you just be friends with them." I replied.

She hung up the phone and that was the last phone call I got from her. I was indeed heart sick. In trying to help these marvelous pioneers I had hurt them instead. This weighed very heavy on my heart and many the night I brooded over this, and vowed to Bahá'u'lláh that I would try to make amends. So the following winter I made arrangements to go back to the town and this time, stay long enough to do significant work. I was given ten days to take the teaching team back there. I phoned this angel of Abhá and told her on the phone that we were coming back and her husband would be home with his family for ten days. I fully expected her to tell me to go straight to hell and please don't ever come back.

I also told her that I would fly in, in a few days and make all the arrangements for the team's arrival and stay. To my surprise she seemed enthusiastic and asked me if I wanted to meet with the Local Spiritual Assembly or with the community. I told her to invite the community.

'Abdu'l-Bahá

Instruction :

> *"Briefly, all effort and exertion put forth by man from the fullness of his heart is worship, if it is prompted by the highest motives and the will to do service to humanity. This is worship: to serve mankind and to minister to the needs of the people."*

> *PT 176-177*

That evening when I walked into her living room, I counted 19 Bahá'ís. All the arrangements were speedily made and these firm and dedicated souls all participated and helped with everything, from housing to meals. Then our hostess left for the kitchen to make refreshments. I turned to these Bahá'ís in amazement and asked what had happened. This was unheard of in the entire field of teaching. Even back in the late 1920's and early 30's, when a new Bahá'í had to read seven books and then pass a most difficult test to become a Bahá'í, we still did not get 100%. Yet here in this town, this woman, all by herself, had achieved the impossible.

"This woman is an angel," one man responded. "When this woman came to see me, I told her that I was not interested in religion and I don't know what possessed me to sign that card. I had gone to the bar one night. It was bitterly cold and I drank too much and became drunk. When the bar closed, the streets were deserted and I started for home, but I was too drunk and started to pass out. Even in my drunken stupor, I fully realized that if I passed out, that in just a very short time I would be a block of ice and this would be my final sleep. I also knew in my subconscious that I was going. All of a sudden, this big Cadillac car pulled up alongside me, this lady in a fur coat got out, and pulled and tugged and got me into her car. She then took me up here to her house and poured coffee into me. As I sobered up, she not only saved my physical life but saved my spiritual life as well. She taught me all about Bahá'u'lláh. That woman is an angel. I owe her a debt I can never repay."

Another woman spoke up and said, "Let me tell you what happened with me. This lady came to my house and it was freezing cold. I didn't even invite her in but she handed me her card and said if I ever needed any thing to give her a call and she left. It was a couple of weeks later and I woke up in the morning with the most horrible migraine headache I had ever had. When I tried to get up I almost vomited.

The children had to be gotten up, fed and sent to school, the baby was crying and messy and my husband had already gone to work. It took all my strength to just call the phone number on the card. In 10 minutes this woman was in my house. She fed, dressed and got the children off to school. She cleaned up and fed the baby. She cleaned up my kitchen, made the beds and put on the laundry. She stayed with me all day and even fixed dinner for my children and husband. As my headache went away this angel of God told me the beautiful story of Bahá'u'lláh, which went right to my heart. I love this woman with all my heart and can never thank her sufficiently for what she has done for me and my family."

So each and every soul in that community had a similar story to tell of service, service and more service. Surely this is a grand example:

Bahá'u'lláh

Instruction :

> *"Say, O brethren! Let deeds not words be your adorning."*

HWP #5

So, dear friends, if you want 100% in your consolidation efforts here is the only way I have ever seen it happen. One of the things that stands out clearly here is that this Cause of God has always demanded a high degree of sacrifice, like the above story shows. Just imagine this elegant lady of a very high social position dragging a drunk into her car or going herself to clean up somebody else's mess.

CHAPTER 14

THE MYSTERY OF SACRIFICE

'Abdu'l-Bahá

Instruction :

"How many were the individuals who sacrificed their own personal advantage and out of desire to please the Lord devoted the days of their lives to teaching the masses."

SDC-85

What 'Abdu'l-Bahá said about sacrifice, of course, is really true and that is: it is impossible to sacrifice. It is like the caterpillar sacrificing itself to become the multi-colored beautiful butterfly or the flower sacrificing itself to become the fruit. Yet, we as lovers of the Blessed Beauty, must make every effort to sacrifice our all in His path. I long with all my heart, soul and inmost being to be able to sacrifice something to Bahá'u'lláh, and after 40 years of strenuous service, my desire goes unfulfilled. I give Him a drop and He returns to me the ocean. I give Him a moment and He gives me an eternity. Let's give a few concrete real life examples.

The time was at the start of the Guardian's Ten Year Crusade. I had quit a very good position, sold my junk, and with my wife and three babies headed off to the birth place of the winds, the Aleutian Islands, a goal of the plan. One of the babies was 4 years old, one was 2 years old, and one was 3 weeks old. I had contended that the Aleuts lived there, so we would live as they did. I had visions of myself in a kayak chasing whale around the Bering Sea.

Upon my arrival, however, my dream was shattered, as the Aleut people, for the most part, were wards of the government and on government relief and we did not qualify. There was no work of any kind and our cash reserves were fast dwindling away. No one on earth, except us, knew the dire circumstances of our position. Yet our beloved Guardian, drawing upon that unique inspiration that was his, and his alone, sent us the instructions that we "must accept financial help from the American Bahá'í community." Only God knows how he knew, for we had told no one. After much prayer and consultation we decided to sacrifice this sorely needed aid and wrote the Guardian, "Please, Shoghi Effendi, not that, we cannot face taking from the fund that we long to support. Maybe our sacrifice of this badly needed assistance will inspire the American Bahá'ís to wipe out once and for all that annual deficit." Amátu'l-Bahá Rúhíyyih Khánum sent us a very loving letter in reply, and she said that we had made Shoghi Effendi very, very happy. Now one of the last instructions of `Abdu'l-Bahá was to make the Guardian happy.

'Abdu'l-Bahá

Instruction :

> *"O ye the faithful loved ones of `Abdu'l-Bahá! It is incumbent upon you to take the greatest care of Shoghi Effendi. . . that no dust of despondency may stain his radiant nature, that day by day he may wax greater in happiness, in joy and spirituality, and may grow to become even a fruitful tree."*

PP-44

This, of course, did not alleviate our financial situation. Starting in September, a terrible storm moved in. Ice, snow, rain and sleet, backed up by winds of hurricane forces, lashed the island constantly all though October, November, and up into December. One of the things about a remote Island is that when the tide goes out the table is set. In our case, however, it was worth your life to attempt to go out in this storm. My wife told me one day that we could not possibly make it. One thing about my wife, she was an extremely practical woman and when she said we couldn't make it, for sure we couldn't make it. So we sat down with our prayer books and consulted. The thought of leaving our Crusader post never entered our minds.

It was decided that starting in the morning, no more breakfasts, and then in the next few days we would ration out the food. Full rations for the children as they had no say in being there, but for us we would now starve for Bahá'u'lláh. I remember how happy I was with this decision. In my bed that night I was thinking, "Now, Bahá'u'lláh, finally I will sacrifice something to you. I may even be allowed to starve." This storm that had assaulted the Island for over 3 months, died down and stopped as we slept.

In the morning, my wife was in the kitchen fixing breakfast for the babies and someone knocked loudly on the door. I opened the door and a man all covered with snow was standing there. He said, "I come from Dutch Harbor (another island) and I work for Standard Oil. This storm has taken out our power lines and we have no electricity. I understand that you are an Electrical Engineer and would you like a job."

I replied, "Come in, come in. Yes, of course, I will take the job. But you must understand that I am not a true electrician but I know I can fix your power lines." In fact when I put on my first pair of telephone pole spurs, I put them on the outside of my shoe.

Then I shouted to the kitchen, "Ma, put on breakfast."

You see, Bahá'u'lláh would not even let me give Him my breakfast. From that point forward I had all of the money we needed and ended up with a big business in the Aleutians.

'Abdu'l-Bahá

Instruction :

> ". . . *those who proclaim their longing to make great sacrifices can only prove their truth by their deeds.*"

PT-50

During the nine-year plan one of the goals in Mexico was to have at least one Bahá'í in each state of Mexico. Our goal was the state of Oaxaca and by just living there the goal was won. As I was self supporting from my Aleutian Island cannery, I resolved to try to open at least nine new centers. Using a map of the state and a ruler I chose a spot that seemed to be about five miles from the highway as the primary target for the teaching work. The name of the village was Zoquiapan, as it turned out, the five miles were the way a crow would fly and I was not a crow. It ended up being about fifteen miles and over three mountains. The name of those mountains are the Sierra Madras, which means, mother mountains. Those of us that had the privilege of hiking in them we will most assuredly agree, that they are indeed the mother mountains. .

The reason I chose the place off of the Highway was because we have learned that the further you can get away from this so-called civilization and commercialization the more receptive are the natives. A young Spanish speaking woman from Venezuela was coming to help me and I was going into Zoquiapan to make the arrangements for her visit.

So I hiked, and I hiked, and I hiked, zig-zagging up one mountain and zig-zagging down the other side, around the streams and rivers and up another mountain and so on. Every muscle in my body began to ache with the unheard of exertion. My toe nail cut over into my toe and it began to bleed, as I struggled, the dirt of the trail worked into the wound and a severe infection set in.

At this point, I determined that Bahá'u'lláh said, "make an effort", but this was too much. So as I neared the village I determined, even if my Spanish was rudimentary, I would give the message and bug out of there and never come back.

The people of Zoquiapan were the most receptive souls I had ever encountered up to that time. They were so eager, and began asking me questions that I did not understand. So I told them,

" OK, I'll come back and I will bring with me a girl who speaks Spanish and she will answer all your questions." The response was magnetic. "Will you really come back?" "No one ever comes to see us." "We won't go to our fields, we will wait for you." "For sure you will come back?"

I responded with, "God willing. I will be back next Saturday." As they were so insistent I also added, "Si Dios Quiera." If God wants, and "O'hallah", which is the Spanish equivalent of the Arabic, En Shah Allah.

If the hike into the village was terrible, the hike out was much worse. By the time I returned to the city of Oaxaca, the infection in my foot had spread and my foot was swollen up. The foot was soaked and the toenail trimmed. The infection got worse and by Friday, just going to the bathroom, was excruciating pain. I was on the bed and told myself, "You said God willing and it is very evident that God is not willing. I can't even walk."

I said a Tablet of Aḥmad, closed my eyes and was instantly back in the village of Zoquiapan with those beaming and interested people. Once more I could hear the voices saying, "No one ever visits us. Will you really come back?" Then I was back on the bed. "OK, Bahá'u'lláh, tomorrow I will sacrifice for those people and will go back to Zoquiapan." Just the thought of being able to finally sacrifice something to Bahá'u'lláh filled me with an untold happiness. I told myself, "Now, after all these years, I will give something to Him. I would give Him my pain, and if I had to crawl on my hands and knees over three mountains, I would not disappoint those people. One thing, along with learning that the secret of sacrifice is that there is no sacrifice, is also learning that the Cause of God is built on our making the effort to sacrifice. If there is no sacrifice, there will be no victories and this is a truth borne out from the first breath of the glorious Báb to the present day, and we can be assured that this truth will last for the thousand years as foretold by Bahá'u'lláh.

The following morning at dawn found us on the mountain and as we struggled up the first mountain, I looked at my companion. She was a fat girl and with each step she was struggling and puffing up this extremely steep mountain. Tears were running down her face and she said, "I can't, I can't, I can't." I felt with each step pain clear to my shoulder. I echoed her words, "I can't, I can't, I can't."

"Come sit down," I said. "Let's pray." We sat on the boulders at the side of the trail and prayed.

'Abdu'l-Bahá

Instruction :

"O Lord my God and my Haven in my distress! My Shield and my Shelter in my woes! My Asylum and Refuge in time of

need   and   in   my   loneliness   my Companion!...."

BP-30

Never before had this prayer been said with such heart felt feeling. Thewords seemed to take on new meaning and stirred us to our depths. We got up, without a word to each other, continued up the mountain still struggling against the pain. At the top of the mountain my companion said, "Oh! Oh! Oh! what a beautiful place, I feel as if God is right here with us." I looked at her and she was transfigured. She was beaming with radiant light and I knew that the spirit of Bahá'u'lláh had joined us on that mountain top. He said to our souls, "It is all right my children. I will walk with you now." We began to sing the Greatest Name, like a cascading waterfall, the sound seemed to flow out and around the mountain and encompassed us. It is God's truth that I don't remember any pain from that point on into the village. I seemed to be walking on air. The questions that I did not understand from my previous visit were, "How can we become Bahá'ís?"

Yes, it is truly impossible to sacrifice anything for the Cause of God. From many such experiences I have come to the conclusion that God is never going to be in man's debt and we will be forever in His.

CHAPTER 15

THE GREATEST GIFT

I think the attitude of really loving and caring for the people that the teacher is trying to teach is another essential for successful teaching. I learned this well in India.

'Abdu'l-Bahá

Instruction :

"Be thou a summoner to love, and be thou kind to all the human race. Love thou the children of men and share in their sorrows."

SWA-26

There was a nine-day institute that I was to do in a village called Panchgani, where the New Era Bahá'í school is located. On the road from Bombay to Poona, the car broke down. We got into a so-called auto mechanic's yard at the side of the road. This mechanic had a 12 inch crescent wrench and he began by tapping the spark plugs with this wrench. I could not watch, so I walked away and out of his yard. Suddenly I heard someone wailing and crying as if her heart would break. I followed the sound over to a ditch. Down in this ditch was a little woman. She was in rags, she was sobbing with excruciating pain of heart and soul. I went back to the car, got my translator took him over to this ditch and asked, "What is wrong with this woman?"

My translator, who was conversant with most of the dialects in India, spoke with the woman, who replied through her sobs that her son had died about six weeks ago and she was weeping for her son.

My heart was moved to its depths, as one could see from her condition that she had almost washed her eyes out of her head with her crying, they were so red and sunken. I told the translator, "OK, that is enough, she has wept enough and her son, who is still in existence, he does not want her to weep any more." Now, just because somebody cared, really cared, you could feel some of her grief lift away, but only a little. So I continued, through my translator, to explain about life after death. God had transplanted her precious son to a garden of light and happiness· from this dark and sad world of pain and suffering.

More of her grief lifted off, and her anguish of heart began to ease off. I then explained that this separation from her child was only temporary and it was a fact, from the mouth of Bahá'u'lláh, that she would, in the future, be reunited with him. More of the bitter anguish was dissipated. She was still weeping, however. I told my translator to tell her again that her son was all right and that I would pray for the soul of her son and for her. When this was translated the woman stopped crying altogether and looked at me very intently as I read the prayer for the departed. When I finished I jumped down into the ditch, took her hand, looked into her eyes and said in English, "Your son is all right."

She smiled, a deep heartfelt smile and nodded her head and went on her way. In a land of over eight hundred million people, nobody cared. As Bahá'ís we must not only care, but must take the action to show the children of men that we do truly care and we must do this in our everyday life.

Bahá'u'lláh

Instruction :

"Religion bestoweth upon man the most precious of all gifts, offereth the cup of prosperity, imparteth eternal life, and showereth imperishable benefits upon mankind."

TB-130

Another very important principle that is brought into play in these instances of loving and caring for people is, The Greatest Gift is the gift of teaching. Many people ask the question, "What is this going to do for me?" The answer is that it cannot only bring an element of peace and consolation to a heart, as the above story clearly shows, but it can also be the means of a complete transformation of people's lives as the following example will clearly show.

We were just coming out of Zoquiapan where we had some new Bahá'ís enter the Cause. I had a badly infected foot and my companion was over weight. We knew we were going to have to come back again and again in order to follow the instruction of, "not leaving the new found friends to their own devices." Now, a 15-mile hike each way may not seem so much to a mountaineer, but I can vouch for the fact that it is almost too much for the average person like me. More so when it is over 3 mountains with an infected foot.

At about the halfway point, with the mid-day sun beating down and us needing water, a small adobe house came into view on the mountainside up ahead. I told my companion that this had to be a Bahá'í home, in the future, we would have to stop for water and rest as we came and went to Zoquiapan. So we came to the door and knocked. A little old man opened the door. His eyes were dead, that is he was living in some remote past. His life time of innate courtesy made him invite us in. I could sense at once that it was an intrusion into his privacy and he did not want us. I ached all over and thought that I would rest in the shade for just a few minutes, then get some water, excuse ourselves and leave.

My companion, who was a Spanish speaker, whom I had just told on the trail that this had to be a Bahá'í house, began at once to explain about Bahá'u'lláh and to give the message. This little man sat there with his lifeless eyes, every time the teacher would pause and ask him what he thought, he would reply, "Si como no." which means, yeah, why not. I sat in the shade, drank some water and rested my aching body. I knew that this man was not even listening to her and felt ashamed of myself for not leaving at once.

As this man seemed to agree with everything the teacher said, she finally asked the big question, "Would you like to be a Bahá'í?" To which he replied, "Yeah, why not." She got out her pen and the enrollment card and asked him if he could fill it in. For the first time his eyes showed some life, for a moment he came back to the present. "No, I am an ignorant man. I can't read or write," he said.

"Never mind," she explained. "I will fill it in for you. What is your name?"

Fear and consternation filled this man's face and he was now fullyawake. I am sure he thought we were the tax collectors. "My name," he stammered, "Why do you want my name?"

"Well, you have agreed with everything I said and you said that you believe in Bahá'u'lláh, so you are a Bahá'í, I will fill out the card for you."

The fear went out of his face and he gave her his name. Now, I had sat through this whole seemingly farce of a situation and felt very bad. So I went up to this little unhappy man, took him into my arms, gave him a very warm hug (abrazo) and told him we loved him very much. Then my companion took his hand, with a glowing face welcomed him into the Cause of God.

This little man stepped back and said, "Just a minute, that name I gave you is not my name. I just made up a name. I want my real name on the card." What had happened to Don Mario was that his wife had died and he was left alone with his grown and married children. He wanted to die also, but was afraid of death. He had become so unhappy and filled with remorse that the family had moved away. Here he was alone, unloved, unwanted, wanting to die, but afraid of death and very miserable. Now that his heart and mind were open and receptive, this little angel that was with me, truly filled his heart with the love of Bahá'u'lláh. When we left we gave him a prayer book and again he said, "I'm an ignorant man. I don't read. I don't write, so what good is a book for me?" I asked him if any of his family could read, when he assured me that his daughter-in-law Pascuala could read, I told him to take her the prayer book, marked off the short obligatory prayer for him and explained how she could help him memorize this prayer by him repeating it after his daughter-in-law.

Bahá'u'lláh

Instruction :

> *"Blessed the ignorant one who seeketh the fountain of My knowledge;"*

TB-16

The following month, when I stopped to see Don Mario, I asked him if he really wanted to be a Bahá'í.

He replied with glowing eyes, "Yes, and already I am telling all the people on the mountain about Bahá'u'lláh."

"What about the prayer? Did you memorize it?"

"No, I went to my daughter-in-law like you said, and at first she tried to help me. She would read a line and I would say the line, but soon she was reading the prayers herself to God and she forgot all about me, so I took my prayer book and I went home."

He gave me directions to his daughter-in-law's house and I determined to go see this woman, who got so into the prayers that she forgot her father-in-law. When I found the place, it was little more than a hovel. There were some tree branches piled up against one wall of crumbling adobe. Outside were two naked babies with tummies swollen up from starvation. Their arms and legs were like toothpicks and their eyes were the universal eyes of near death, starving children. I crawled in under the tree branches and found a woman of about 21 years old. She was on her knees with two stones, trying to grind up a handful of corn to put some corn mush into her babies mouths to keep them alive. Her dress was a rag that we would not even use to clean the floor. My heartfelt reaction was "Oh God! How poor is my little sister."

When Pascuala learned who I was, her eyes glowed like diamonds and her face beamed with light. She never just said the words God, Jesus, Christ or Bahá'u'lláh. She said these words with so much love and sincerity that they shook me from the soles of my feet to the top of my head. I was only in her presence for a few minutes and I was saying, "Oh God! How rich is my little sister." I would give all I possess for just a small amount of her love, devotion and sincerity before God.

She told me how deeply the prayers had touched her inmost being and how she knew that these words had come from God Himself. Her father-in-law had told her about Bahá'u'lláh and she knew He was true. I explained that if she believed in Bahá'u'lláh, she was a Bahá'í and I would enroll her. She stopped me and said that she could not be a Bahá'í because her husband was a drunk and if he found out she was a Bahá'í he would beat her. Living with her husband, she told me, was like living with an animal. I then explained that being a Bahá'í was between her heart and Bahá'u'lláh, if she did not want to sign a card that was not as important as her heart and the feelings of her heart. I then gave her a prayer book and told her that no one except Bahá'u'lláh, her and I would know that she was a Bahá'í. I have never in my life given a gift to anyone that gave them as much joy and happiness as that prayer book I gave to Pascuala. She clutched it to her breast, when she realized that I was giving it to her, tears came into her eyes, tears of joy, for now she could talk to God using His words, words that fed and touched the heart. I also wanted to reach into my pocket and give her some money to feed her starving babies. However, I remembered the instructions about not mixing material gifts with the teaching work and I didn't do it. My heart was not at peace with this, but it still is, "FOLLOW THE INSTRUCTIONS" even if you do not fully understand them.

Universal House of Justice

Instruction:

> *"When teaching among the masses, the friends should be careful not to emphasize the charitable and humanitarian aspects of*

*the Faith. . . .even when clothes and food are
offered to the people being taught, many
complications arise."*

WG-32

Bahá'u'lláh

Instruction :

*"The poor in your midst are My trust;
guard ye My trust,"*

HWP-54

Bahá'u'lláh

Instruction :

"Bestow My wealth upon My poor,"

HWA-57

This seems to be a conflict and you can understand why
my heart was not at peace. However, upon reflection the
wealth of Bahá'u'lláh is His teachings. The greatest gift.
Also in consultation with Amátu'l-Bahá Rúhíyyih Khánum
we talked about rice Bahá'is, which is people that become
Bahá'is only for the rice given to them.

The following month, as I was going to Zoquiapan, I
stopped in to see Pascuala. She told me that she was very
much afraid of her husband, for he was an alcoholic and like
an animal, but she was more afraid of God. So she would
sign the card like all the other Bahá'ís on the mountain. I
tried to tell her that this was not needed but she insisted.
I gave her the card and she filled it in and signed it. She
then began to gather up her rags and stones and things. Then
she said, "I am going to run away from home because my
husband is an animal and he will beat me. Anyway, I was
going to run away and now I must."

"Wait! Wait!" I cried. "You can't do that. You are a Bahá'í and now you must do the things Bahá'u'lláh wants you to do. You must be more loving, kind, gentle, giving, forgiving, truthful, honest and faithful to your husband."

Her eyes got bigger and bigger and she blurted out, "You mean God wants me to be like that with an animal? Look how I am forced to live and look at my babies. If God wants I will try."

I responded, "Yes, you must try. Yes, God wants." Then I heaved a great sigh of relief and left.

The following month as I came singing down the trail, Pascuala heard me and ran out to meet me. She explained, "I told my husband that I am a Bahá'í and he didn't beat me." I also learned later, that up until she became a Bahá'í, every time her husband came home drunk she would light into him like Tarzan going after the apes. "You dirty, drunken, stupid man look how I live, look at your children, look at these rags I have to wear, look at how we live." and on and on until he beat her and passed out on the mat. This time he came home and she tried to be loving, kind and understanding. She didn't say anything. She took off his muddy boots when he passed out on the mat and covered him up with a rag they called a blanket.

This situation went on for about a year. Then one month as I came down the trail her husband was waiting for me.

"Do you think God will answer the prayer of an angel?" he asked.

"Yes, I am sure He will," I answered.

"Well then I am going to be a Bahá'í."

"For you," I explained, "That will be very difficult as you know Bahá'u'lláh said that you cannot drink alcohol."

"You said God would answer the prayer of an angel and my wife Pascuala is an angel and she said she would pray for me. Will you pray for me too? I will also pray very hard."

"Yes, of course I will, I will pray for you everyday."

"I think God will answer your prayer also and I have a plan. Tomorrow I will get up before dawn and go to my field and I will work in my field until I drop over at night. If I need something from the village I will send Pascuala, because if I go I know I can't help myself and I will start drinking again. Do you think this is a good plan and that God and Bahá'u'lláh will help me?" he asked.

I assured him that it was a wonderful plan and we would all pray for his success.

The second year went by and I would see Pascuala and the children taking lunch out to the field where her husband worked from dawn to dark every day. Soon he had the most productive and beautiful field in those parts of the mountain.

'Abdu'l-Bahá

Instruction:

> *"Of all the gifts of God the greatest is the gift of Teaching. It draweth unto us the Grace of God and is our first obligation. Of such a gift how can we deprive ourselves?"*

BA-12

One day as I was going into Zoquiapan, the husband was waiting for me on the trail. He had on a new hat, new white shirt, new white pants and new sandals. He stopped me and said that they were having a fiesta (party) for me at his house. I told him that I liked parties and I started down the trail toward his shack. He stopped me and said that the party was not there. I followed him around the mountain and up to a brand new adobe house. Pascuala was there with a new dress, high heel shoes and nylons. The two children were also dressed in new clothes, their little bodies filled out and their eyes and faces filled with joy as they played with some new toys.

Now this man and his family walk upon the earth with dignity, heads high and eyes clear. Was not the Cause of Bahá'u'lláh indeed the greatest gift? I look back to the time I first met Pascuala and how I longed to give her some money, and I think of the consequences. If I had given her the money that first time, I am sure her husband would have come home drunk, found her with food and money and asked her where she got it. He would have beaten her and taken the money and, the next month, he would have been hiding in the bushes and forcing Pascuala to beg for her children. I thank God for the wisdom of the instructions. The result is light upon light and, even as this incidence proves it is indeed THE GREATEST GIFT, THE GIFT OF TEACHING. Even as to the material benefits, not just the spiritual ones, this following the instructions bring undreamed of benefits.

CHAPTER 16

LOVE COMES FROM BAHÁ'U'LLÁH

I have mentioned before, but again would like to reinforce this concept of giving credit to Bahá'u'lláh. We have had great difficulties with new teachers that join the mass teaching projects. When they first come, they are humble and insecure and as a result their prayers are sincere and from their hearts. They go out to teach with only the support and complete confidence in the promises of the Blessed Beauty.

Báb

Instruction:

"Arise in His name, put your trust wholly in Him, and be assured of ultimate victory."

TDP-3

They do indeed lay all of their affairs in God's hands. So of course they are most successful and are able to touch the hearts of the ones they come in contact with. Then they come in and think, "Well now that wasn't so hard, I did good. Just look at these new believers." This attitude brings this teacher down from the spiritual high, like sliding down a fireman's pole. The next time they go out they find they have little or no success and they will ask, "What happened to me? I was doing so well before." It is harder to get them back up than it was to get them up the first time.

This has happened to me. I would go to a place and my motive would be absolutely pure. Just for Bahá'u'lláh, only for Bahá'u'lláh, and no other purpose. Then, as I got into the area and truly loved the people, with that true and divine love inspired by Bahá'u'lláh, the people would shower upon me so much love in return, that I would lose my purity of motive and find myself going back into the area just for the wonderful love the people were giving to me. It is not being suggested that you love the people less, no, in fact you will love them even more if you can be doing it for Bahá'u'lláh.

Bahá'u'lláh

Instruction:

> *"Take pride not in love for yourselves but in love for your fellow-creatures."*

TB-138

Why do you teach? The answer is because you love the people so much that you long with all your heart to share with your loved ones the greatest gift, in order to bring them that deep, soul satisfying happiness you have found.

The real truth in loving people is the fact that we must love them into the Faith of God. As I travel from country to country and community to community and I ask the question, "How did you become a Bahá'í ?" The answer most of the time is, "When I walked into that place I felt such a wonderful love and spirit." This is a truth that no one can deny.

Bahá'u'lláh

Instruction :

> *"Be most loving one to another."*

Gl-316

So the teacher must get it firmly in mind that we are going out to love people into the Cause of God. When we do truly love the people, then we are truly interested in them and are willing to listen very carefully to what they have to say.

I was up in the northern part of New York state at the home of a very warm-hearted and loving Bahá'í couple. I noticed his neighbor out in the yard and asked this Bahá'í if he had ever given the message to his neighbor. He said that he had mentioned it to him and had often invited him to his home for firesides but he showed no interest and this man had never been in his home. I walked over to the fence and introduced myself to this neighbor and explained that I was a visiting Bahá'í. Then I began to just talk to the man about this that and the other thing. As I asked questions with real love and concern and in no time we were like long lost friends and brothers that had become reunited. He was sharing with me all of his deepest problems of life and I in turn was gently giving him the Bahá'í solutions to his problems. Somebody cared, just like the woman in India, someone loved him.

My host called me to come to dinner and so I invited this neighbor to come along and he did. Not only did he come for dinner but stayed on for the fireside and was the last one to leave when the evening finished.

'Abdu'l-Bahá

Instruction :

> *"O thou son of the Kingdom! All things are beneficial if joined with the love of God:"*

SAB-181

The real power of this divine love once manifested in the believer's life has the power to change the planet. For five thousand years of recorded history every messenger of God has told us to love each other. We have written books, held conferences and talked about it for all this time, but we have never done it. We have never followed the instructions. In fact we have done just the opposite. We have hated and killed and warred with each other. Let us make a solemn vow to God that we will try it. If we don't like loving each other we can always return to hating and killing each other. Then daily let's pray, "O God! give me a loving heart. Make my heart overflow with love for thy creatures." Believe me the results of just the Bahá'ís making this vow and striving to incorporate it into their lives will change the world over night.

Bahá'u'lláh

Instruction:

> *"The brightness of the fire of your love will no doubt fuse and unify the contending peoples and kindreds of the earth, whilst the fierceness of the flame of enmity and hatred cannot but result in strife and ruin."*

Gl-96

It was the last four months of the nine-year plan and I had just come out of India. As usual when I was any where near to Israel, I would stop for a three-day visit, go to the shrines and thank Bahá'u'lláh for His blessings and beseech Him for my future protection. When I entered the Pilgrim House, Hand of the Cause Dr. Rahmatu'lláh Muhájir was talking to Hand of the Cause 'Alí Akbar Furútan in the middle of the room. When Hand of the Cause Dr. Rahmatu'lláh Muhájir saw me he motioned for me to come to him.

He said, "Jenabe, you are now going to Germany."

"No, Dr. Muhájir I am not going to Germany." I replied, "I am going home to Alaska. I have been out now for over six months and I am going home."

Hand of the Cause Dr. Rahmatu'lláh Muhájir went right on, "We are now down to the last 4 months of the nine-year plan and Germany has not won any of its numerical goals of the plan. The only way they can possibly win their goals is by mass teaching. You are a mass teacher so you are going to Germany."

Hand of the Cause Dr. Rahmatu'lláh Muhájir then took out a note pad and wrote a telegram to the National Assembly of Germany, which he showed me. "Last opportunity to win goals nine year plan. Mass teaching, mass teacher Jenabe Caldwell arriving. Give every support. Dr. Muhájir."

I remonstrated with him, "Dr. Muhájir, I will need at least the three months to get my teachers and train them to do the teaching."

Undaunted he replied, "Bring your Alaskans. They are already trained."

"Dr. Muhájir," I cried. "It will take a fortune to bring over the Alaskan Bahá'ís to Germany."

"Go to Hamburg," he calmly explained, "They will give you the money."

Still unconvinced, I responded, "Dr. Muhájir if I go to Hamburg they won't even give me the time of day let alone their money."

"You go to Hamburg and they will give you the money," he insisted.

I went to Germany and I met with the National Spiritual Assembly of the Bahá'ís of Germany. First they wanted to know what was the first step to be taken by them. I explained that the first step would be putting together a teaching team and we would need some German Bahá'ís willing to give three or four months to the teaching work. I suggested that the National Spiritual Assembly sit down together and draft a real love letter to every enrolled Bahá'í in Germany, requesting that they come for three or four months. I asked that divine institution to write the letter together, not to just give it to the secretary to write. I strongly felt that such a letter would require the inspiration promised by Bahá'u'lláh to that body in full consultation. Their unanimous decision was that they would be wasting their stamps as they explained that they had great difficulty in getting the friends to come to a Saturday night pot luck. I responded that I might not want to come to a pot luck, but might come for the spiritual conquest of Germany. They agreed to try it and I assured them that if no one came, I would go on by myself. They then wanted to know how I planned to do the mass teaching in Germany. I told them that the only way I knew how to do it was to go out and meet the people and talk to them. They assured me that this approach in Germany would not work as people did not talk to strangers in Germany. I explained that I did not know any other way to teach the Faith without talking to the people. They then agreed (only because Hand of the Cause Dr. Rahmatu'lláh Muhájir had instructed them to support this effort) to let me try street teaching in Germany.

Bahá'u'lláh

Instruction :

"All-praise and glory be to God Who, through the power of His might, hath delivered His creation from the nakedness of

> *non-existence, and clothed it with the*
> *mantle of life."*

Gl-77

I would like to pause here in this narrative to make an important point. We the Bahá'ís limit the power of Bahá'u'lláh by our own negative feelings. The power that put the sun in orbit has the supreme power to do anything. Bahá'u'lláh has given mankind all it needs to build the kingdom of God on earth, but He has made it a—Do it yourself kit—. and assured us of His unfailing aid if we will just "follow the instructions."

Bahá'u'lláh

Instruction :

> *"Whoso openeth his lips in this Day and maketh mention of the name of his Lord, the hosts of Divine inspiration shall descend upon him from the heaven of My name, the All-Knowing the All-Wise. On him shall also descend the Concourse on high, each bearing aloft a chalice of pure light."*

Gl-280

I then went on to Hamburg and there was a large community of very wealthy Persians in Hamburg. I guess Hand of the Cause Dr. Rahmatu'lláh Muhájir had asked them to come. That evening they all came and donated over $30,000.U.S. Then I went on to Alaska and got 15 God intoxicated lovers and well-trained soldiers in Bahá'u'lláh's army of light. These were all battle scarred veterans from Alaska's Massive Encounter. Their way and expenses were paid so none of the Hamburg money was needed and this was returned to the National Spiritual Assembly of Germany.

We started our program with a teacher training course. I waited to see if any of the German friends would come. First a young man walked in.

I greeted him and inquired, "How is it that you came for such a long time?"

He explained, "You know I got this beautiful love letter from my National Spiritual Assembly. When I read it, I felt like it was a love letter from God, and He was asking me to come for 3 or 4 months. Now tell me how could I refuse?"

"What did you have to do to come?" I asked.

"Well," he said, "I had to drop out of my University and I had only 3 months left to go to get my degree. This means next fall I must go back, pay again the tuition, and do the whole thing over again."

When this beautiful spiritual lad explained what he had done, I knew in my heart that we had won the goals of the nine-year plan. One thing I know for sure and that is this Cause of God is built on sacrifice. If there is no sacrifice, believe me there will be no victory.

'Abdu'l-Bahá

Instruction :

> *"The moth is a sacrifice to the candle. The spring is a sacrifice to the thirsty one. The sincere lover is a sacrifice to the loved one and the longing one is a sacrifice to the beloved."*

TAB-354

Another lady walked in and I asked. "What happened to bring you here?"

She answered, "I got this beautiful love letter asking me to come and I went right over to the phone and called my neighbor and asked her to feed my cats, and here I am.

Another man came in and I asked the same question.

"I got this letter and I went to my boss and asked for time off and he told me that it was a good time as business was slow. So here I am."

The next one explained, "I asked for time off and the boss said no way, so I quit and here I am."

The next, "I got this very beautiful love letter and I called my mother-in-law and told her to feed her son and take care of the grandchildren. I was going on a nine-year plan and would be gone for three months."

So they came from every corner of Germany. Self sacrificing, spiritual souls for a total of 45 front line German soldiers and the 15 Alaskans. I still was at a loss as to what these Alaskans could do in Germany as not one of them spoke German. We had a team of 60 God intoxicated angels of Bahá'u'lláh.

During the teacher training institute, they wanted to know how we were going to go about it and when I explained that we were going out on the streets in Germany and tell the people about Bahá'u'lláh the Germans were aghast, one and all they told me that this could not be done in a country like Germany. As I had told their National Spiritual Assembly, I told them that in all my life I have never been able to teach anyone without talking to them. These Germans were something very special. They did not like the idea, and they were sure it would not work, but they were willing to have a go at it anyhow.

We must also bear in mind that this Cause of God started on May 22nd 1844 with a street teacher. The Báb went out of his house walked out to the edge of town and met a stranger and invited him to His house. Then He asked questions, listened and had a fireside. This resulted in the first declaration on May 23rd, 1844.

It was a cold day in February and the snow was on the ground. We arrived at the Frankfurt House of worship at about 4:30 AM. All 60 of us circumambulated this mother temple of Europe, each one saying quietly to themselves the Tablet of Ahmad. Then silently we filed into the building and one by one went to the podium and said a Tablet of Ahmad. Truly it was a lifetime soul enriching experience. We then left the House of Worship just as the sun was coming up.

We had busses and so we went to a dorf. This is like a village in Germany. The Bahá'ís hit the streets and so the program was launched in Germany. That evening the whole team returned with long faces and unhappy reports. One member of the team told me that it was truly awful. He said he had tried to talk to a man and this man grumbled and walked off. The Alaskans explained to me that they felt the trouble was that the love was coming from their heads and not their hearts. So I took them into our hall and we had consultation on love. I read all the tablets of 'Abdu'l-Bahá, I had on love.

'Abdu'l-Bahá

Instruction :

> *"The essence of Bahá'u'lláh's Teaching is all-embracing love, for love includeth every excellence of humankind."*

SAB-66

We had a 24-hour prayer watch, I instructed the team members to pray, to beg, to beseech Bahá'u'lláh for loving hearts when they went to their prayers that night.

The next evening when the team came in, it was transformed. One man told me, "I didn't try to stop everyone on the street as I did yesterday. I just stood on the corner and watched the people coming and going. I saw a man turn the corner several blocks away and I thought to myself, 'I do love that man. He is my brother. I left my job and came here because I love him so much that I want to share with him the most precious thing I have in my life which is the Cause of God.' I no sooner had this inner conviction than I felt such love flowing through me. It was not coming from me, but through me. This love was like a river and it flowed from me and down the street and when it reached this man, he began to smile. I walked towards him. He walked towards me. When we came together, I said, 'Have you ever heard of Bahá'u'lláh? '

"No," he said. "Please tell me."

So I invited him into a coffee shop and everything I said he responded with, "Isn't that wonderful." You could feel this intense divine and spiritual love all around us. After about 2 hours this person asked if he could please be a Bahá'í."

All the team members were glowing and they all had stories similar to this one. In three months all the goals of the nine-year plan were won.

'Abdu'l-Bahá

Instruction :

> *"Make my heart overflow with love for*
> *Thy creatures. . ."*

BP-31

I think every Bahá'í, deep down inside, knows that love is the answer and the secret of successful teaching. If we don't feel this love or are unable to show it, then let's do as the Germans did and supplicate the Blessed Beauty to give us that loving heart.

CHAPTER 17

TEACH EVERY STRATUM

This loving of people is easy when the people are loveable. It is very difficult to love the unloveable ones. These probably need our love more than anyone else. There were only two women that were Bahá'ís in a village, one was about 60 years old and her mother was about 80. Whenever I visited these two old women they were always most loving and kind and I never ever heard them say even one unkind word about anyone. One day their great granddaughter came to me and declared as a Bahá'í. She then told me that not a single day went by that her grandmother and great- grandmother were not persecuted and slandered because they had become Bahá'ís. When I went to these two jewels of Bahá'u'lláh to console them, their only response was that, "It is so hard to be a Bahá'í and love your neighbors, when they are so nasty."

Universal House of Justice

Instruction :

> *"The paramount goal of the teaching work at the present time is to carry the Message of Bahá'u'lláh to every stratum of human society and every walk of life."*

WG-124

One of the instructions that we must take to heart and try to follow is the instruction to teach every strata of human society. With special attention now called for in reaching the leaders and people of capacity and of course minorities. After all, the millionaires are a minority. Some times we are deceived by the package and do not realize that the little ragged unlettered woman is the true leader of the village. She is the one even the mayor and councilmen come to for advice and solutions to their problems.

'Abdu'l-Bahá

Instruction :

> *"The teacher should not see in himself any superiority; he should speak with the utmost kindliness, lowliness and humility, for such speech exerteth influence and educateth the souls."*

SAB-30

We were in the city of Oaxaca in Mexico and a Bahá'í friend and I were going downtown to do street teaching. Sitting on the sidewalk was an old woman. Her dress was ragged and she was bare footed. She watched the people coming and going. Our eyes met and I said to my friend let's stop and talk to this little old lady. My friend responded, "Jenabe, look how old she is. She is probably set in her ways and all you will accomplish is to disturb her. Anyhow what could she do for the Cause except die."

"Never mind," I said. "You go on downtown and I will talk to her and meet you later."

I sat on the sidewalk next to her and asked her if she had heard of Bahá'u'lláh. She said that she had not, and asked me to please tell her. I explained to her about the Light of God once more illuminating the earth with the coming of God's supreme manifestation. She became excited and said, "I knew God wouldn't forget us. What does He want me to do?"

As I began to tell her about the teachings of Bahá'u'lláh she would stop me and tell me what that meant in a real world with real people. This little woman had grandchildren die in her arms. Every pain, every suffering, every joy and every happiness that life had to offer she had experienced first hand and I sat along side of her all afternoon and got one of the best lessons in life and the Bahá'í teachings I had ever received in my life. Thank God I stopped. Not only for her sake, as she became a very devoted Bahá'í and would even drag her children and grandchildren across town in the rain to come to Bahá'í Feast, but for my spiritual education.

Universal House of Justice

Instruction :

"The unsophisticated people of the world— and they form the large majority of its population—have the same right to know of the Cause of God as others."

LG-595

In French speaking Quebec the team was out teaching and I stayed in the compound with my interpreter. All of a sudden there was the roar and scream of a motorcycle with its engine wide open coming into the compound. He spun his bike around and threw gravel all over the place. He had on the leather studded jacket, the helmet and the beard of a typical biker. He jumped off of his motorcycle and asked if this was the place you could hear about Bahá'í. I told him yes and asked my french interpreter to give him the message. In less than 15 minutes this man was signing his enrollment card. Then the interpreter spent the whole afternoon deepening him in the Faith. An important point here is that we are told in the process of enrolling the new friend must be informed of the three central figures of the Faith, laws they must follow and Administration that they must obey. Even if the card is signed at once as in this case the process of enrolling is not completed until all the instructions have been followed. This process may take quite a long time, but complete it we must if we are to be faithful to the covenant.

Universal House of Justice

Instruction :

> "*. . .in the process of declaring themselves they must, in addition to catching the spark of faith, become basically informed about the Central Figures of the Faith, as well as the existence of laws they must follow and an administration they must obey.*"

WG-32

Late that evening as this new Bahá'í was leaving and I shook his hand and I told him that now he was a Bahá'í he had the obligation to teach others. He gave me a big heart felt smile and said, "Right on Man." and tore out of the compound at full throttle once more throwing gravel all over. The next day here he came again this time with two other bikers following and when he got off of his motorcycle he shook my hand and said, "New Bahá'ís I taught them." My interpreter talked to them until late that evening. In about a week we had about 15 bikers both men and women. They all looked like they were straight out of Hell's Angels. In truth they were Bahá'u'lláh's angels.

When we got in our Bahá'í bus to go on to the next town, we had about 10 bikers in front of us and another 10 behind our bus and the bus had the sign on the side and back that said Bahá'í. They escorted us all the way to the next town. Some of the Canadian Bahá'ís were very concerned about our dignity and image, and this was a good test for all of us in that the Cause of Bahá'u'lláh is for everyone. Every strata of human society.

Shoghi Effendi

Instruction :

> *"It is a great mistake to believe that because people are illiterate or live primitive lives, they are lacking in either intelligence or sensibility. On the contrary, they may well look on us with the evils of our civilization, with its moral corruption, its ruinous wars, its hypocrisy and conceit, as people who merit watching with both suspicion and contempt."*

LG-523

One of the goals of the Nine-year Plan was to take the Cause of God to the Seri reservation in Desinboque. The National Spiritual Assembly of Mexico had a nine-year plan conference and asked for volunteers to help win the goals. A young attractive Bahá'í woman, a pioneer from Chile, who had just arrived in Mexico volunteered to go to the Seri reservation. We were delighted, but failed in our duty to give her the support she should of had for such a project. From the conference she took off for Desinboque.

Bahá'u'lláh

Instruction :

> *"Do men think when they say 'We believe' they shall be let alone and not be put to proof?"*

KI 8-9

About a week later this pioneer was back in Mexico City and on her way back to Chile. She had to go off the road about 57 miles from the nearest town and as there were no buses she started to walk in. She had a small suitcase and had only gone several miles when a group of Seri Indians surrounded her. They took her suit case, her watch, her rings and all her clothes and left her in her birthday suit on the beach. There was no physical abuse, but the mental abuse was beyond belief. There was only mesquite and cactus growing so she had nothing to cover herself with. She lost her passport and all her papers also. We never found out how she got back to Mexico City. All she told us was you must never send anyone back into those awful people.

Of course this story went through the Mexican Bahá'í Community like wildfire so when our National Spiritual Assembly wrote our report to the House we did not say anything about the Seri. The House wrote back and thanked us for our report and all the progress we were making on our goals of the nine-year plan and asked what we were doing about the Seri Reservation and this goal must have priority.

At the next conference when volunteers were requested to go to the Seri no one would go. So, although I was up to my neck in my own work, the House of Justice had said the Seri was a priority, I volunteered to go. Then the Auxiliary Board member said, "If you are going, I am going with you." He was a very small Mayan Indian and it was plain that he was going along to protect me.

At the end of the highway we got some food and water and gassed up my truck. Now this truck had saddle tanks, that is one on each side and each tank held about 30 gallons of gasoline. Which ordinarily would be more than enough for a round trip of 114 miles even for my gas guzzler.

Just as we were getting into the truck, two of the wildest looking Indians I had ever seen came walking up from the beach. My first thought was that Bahá'u'lláh had sent them so I introduced myself to them and asked if it would be possible for both of them or even one of them to guide us into Desinboque. They said no as they had come by boat and would have to take the boat back.

One of these fellows had on a pair of pants that were not a pair as one leg of the pants was missing. He had long black hair that stood out from his head. He had a red ribbon tied around his head. He had on a pair of dark glasses that like the pants were not a pair, one glass was gone and the other lens had one broken piece of dark glass in it. Then a strange thing happened, they had been coming up to the store when I intercepted them, but now they turned around and ran back to their boat and took off without going to the store. I thought about the woman from Chile and that they may be rushing back to form a war party.

Before they left however I had asked them if I could see them again and the one with the dark glasses said sure come see me I live in Santa Rosa. I still felt that Bahá'u'lláh had sent them to us.

There was no road or road signs to follow into Desinboque so we had to just follow the tire tracks in the sand and go north. We would come to a place where the tire tracks went off in five different directions. I would say a prayer and follow one of the sets of tracks and if there were five, I made 5 wrong turns. We even tried saying Tablets of Aḥmad with no better success. All day we travelled and late in the evening we arrived at Santa Rosa.

No one lived there it was just a beautiful sandy beach. Then we heard a jeep coming, this was the first car we had heard all day. So I rushed out and stopped it. I asked the man where Santa Rosa was, and he said you just came out of Santa Rosa so I guessed my Seri Indian did not really want to see us.

Then I asked how far was it to Desinboque and the man said about 40 miles. This meant that we had only covered 17 miles all day and used up over half of the gasoline. So I told the man I would have to follow him back into town to get gas. He said that will not be necessary, just go on down this track and stay in the right track and you will come to my place it is called Punto Chueko, tell my son I sent you and he will sell you the gas you need. Now again one can see how our prayers are answered. If we had not gone down all those wrong tracks all day, we would have gone right past Punto Chueko and into Desinboque. After we got gas it was late in the evening and so we decided to spend the night at Punto Chueko.

Suddenly, who should appear but the Seri Indian we had met that morning. He told me to follow him. So off we went down the beach away from Punto Chueko. Again I thought of the woman from Chile. We came to a double ended dory boat and he told me that this was his boat and he was a fisherman. I told him that I was also a fisherman from Alaska and we traded fish stories.

All of a sudden there were about 9 or 10 Seris around the boat and I was trying to explain to them about Bahá'u'lláh. In the meantime the Auxiliary Board Member became anxious as he saw me go off with the Seri Indian so he came running down the beach to save me. He had been a Christian minister and he had a great fireside with these Indians.

Because it was so hot I just put my cot down by the sea and the Mayan slept in the truck. The next morning at about 4:30 A.M. I woke up with someone pushing on my bed. I opened my eyes and there was the Seri Indian, broken glasses and all. He went right on testing the bed and matter of factly told me he was going with us to Desimboque. So after a dip in the bay for a bath, we were off to Desimboque. Now after all these pages of telling you dear reader to listen, carefully listen, I'm afraid I did not follow my own advise. The Indian sat alongside me as I drove and my Bahá'í companion sat in the back seat of the truck. I began to talk about Bahá'u'lláh and I talked and talked and talked some more. When I finally stopped, my normally quite and reserved Mayan friend began to talk and he talked and talked and talked some more. All this time the Indian sat and the only thing he said was, "Turn right, turn left, or go straight, he did not even say yes, no or even grunt.

When we arrived in Desimboque the Indian jumped out of the truck and was gone. A large group of Seris gathered around the truck and they were hostile. They started rocking the truck and they were going to tip it over. I told my friend quick out of the truck as I would rather that they tip me over than the truck as it would be easier to pick myself up than to turn back overthe truck. As we jumped out these Indians came around us and the mood was angry. I said, "We have come here for God."

Instantly the mood changed and they responded, "You talk about God, we like that. please you tell us about God." So the hostility was evaporated. I left my Mayan friend to tell them about Bahá'u'lláh, and I went to fill up the canteens with water. At the water tap I met a beautiful Seri woman and as it turned out she was our Indian's sister. She invited me to her home to tell her and her husband about Bahá'í. Unlike her brother she was very talkative. Her questions were deep, sincere and thoughtful and she took literature to read and invited us back. I was delighted as once you have friends and can return, the place is open to the Cause. In the meantime my Mayan friend had also got a number of very interested Seris. So we bid our new found friends goodby, as we made our final farewells the door of the truck opened and in came our Indian friend.

On our return to Punto Chueko we were all quite with only our friend Jose saying turn here, go straight, go left or turn right. About 5 miles from Punto Chueko, I thought to myself, "You know this Indian, I'm afraid, is not very bright."

At once Jose said, "That's right I am not the smartest Indian up here, a lot of these Indians are a lot smarter than I." I had only had the thought and he spoke.

Then he went on to say, "I am not very smart but I know something that no other Seri in the world knows, and that is that Bahá'u'lláh is true."

I stopped the truck and asked my Mayan friend if he heard what I thought I heard, and he confirmed it. Now, it seemed, we had our first Seri in the Cause of Bahá'u'lláh. I got out the enrollment card and handed it to Jose. He then said, "I have one more question." As if he had been asking questions all the time. He went on to say, "I really like to drink, in fact I just love to get drunk. What do we Bahá'ís believe about that?"

I reached over and took the card back and put it in my pocket. "You know Jose," I explained, "God loves His creation very much, more even than a mother loves her baby. He looks down and he sees men get drunk and hurt their wives. Mothers get drunk and hurt their children. People get drunk and kill innocent people on the highways in their cars. They destroy their minds and bodies with alcohol. So God says to us his children that he loves so much, please don't do that.

Jose looked very thoughtful for a few minutes thinking about what I had told him. Then a big smile came onto his face and he reached across and took the card out of my pocket and said, "OK."

Again I prejudged our new Bahá'í brother, I thought he probably can't write. He immediately filled out and signed the card. Then I asked the Mayan Bahá'í to read a prayer as I again thought this guy couldn't read. Jose reached back, jerked the prayer book out of the Mayan's hand and said, "Give it to me." He read the Bahá'í prayer with absolutely no problem. I was sure now that Jose was reading my mind. We gave him a prayer book and a small framed Greatest Name and Jose was so excited that he jumped out of the truck and with the prayer book in one hand and the Greatest Name in the other, both clutched tightly to his chest, his wild hair in the wind he raced off over the sand.

This story of the first Seri in the Cause of God is a good example of don't judge people by the package they present. We must just go ahead and follow the instructions and teach every strata of human society. Because Jose looked very different I had prejudged him to be wild. I am sure this is what the beloved Guardian Shoghi Effendi meant about us over coming our prejudices.

Shoghi Effendi

Instruction :

> ". . . *and complete freedom from prejudice in their dealing with peoples of a different race, class, creed, or color. . . and none can claim, how ever much he may have progressed along this line, to have completely discharged the stern responsibilities which it inculcates.*"

ADJ-18-19

CHAPTER 18

CULTURAL DIVERSITY

In the process of teaching everyone and not prejudging them we must be ever alert and listen to what they themselves want to do in teaching the Cause. To often we go to different cultures and think we know what is the best for the people of that culture. Even worse we try to impose upon the natives our ideas or our cultural mores.

In the state of Washington, I took on the personal goal of trying to reach the Tualip Indians. I had decided this because it was an easy drive and I had discovered that there were 19 tribes west of the mountains. First I prayed and asked Bahá'u'lláh for His guidance and help. I said tablets of Aḥmad as I drove to the reservation. I asked Bahá'u'lláh to send any hearts that He had prepared to me. Then I told myself that I would stop anyone I met on the street or out in the open and try to make contact with them.

Well I went into the town and I drove up and down the street several times and not one single soul was on the street. So I parked my car and walked through the town and back to my car and never met a single person. So I went to the beach sat on a rock and prayed and thanked Bahá'u'lláh for answering my prayer. I then returned home.

The following week as I went to the reservation I again prayed and this time decided to be more audacious. I would go right to the Indian office and do an open proclamation. You see here was a case of not following the instructions of using wisdom, listening to find out where the person is at, and gently share with them this glorious message.

I walked right into the office met the leader of the reservation and unhesitatingly told him his Lord and Savior Jesus Christ had returned. His mouth dropped open and he was stunned. When he regained his composure, he told me to go find the ministers that were on the reservation and tell them and they would in turn tell the people. I went back to the beach sat on my rock and again thanked Bahá'u'lláh.

A Bahá'í Indian from the Yakima reservation on the other side of the mountains wanted to go over to the Yakima reserve to teach and so I volunteered to take her over. When I picked her up she had another Indian friend who wanted to go with us. His name was Billy and he was a full blood Tualip and when he got in the car he boldly announced that he had a religion and my Bahá'í friend and I started talking to each other. For the first part of the trip Billy just listened but by the second half of the trip he was asking questions a mile a minute and by the time we arrived at the Yakima Reserve Billy was the first Tualip Indian in the cause of God. He was so excited he could not sit still and the first group of Yakima Indians we ran into Billy jumped out of the car and started teaching.

Billy was a wonder to see and his instant love of Bahá'u'lláh was deep and secure. That whole weekend he taught Bahá'í day and night. When he wasn't teaching he was praying and deepening his knowledge of the Cause. On our way home I asked Billy what would be the best way to reach and teach on the Tualip reservation. After some time he decided that the best way would be for the Bahá'ís to hold an international picnic on the reservation. Let the Indians see and feel the Bahá'í love and spirit and in an informal way make friends. Billy said he would arrange it with the tribal leaders, which he did. He picked the time and the place where all the Indians usually gathered on a Sunday. I got on the phone and called all the LSA's in the area and all my personal friends and invited them to the Tualip for Billy's picnic.

One LSA near the Tualip sent a committee out and when they saw the place with the out houses etc. They decided in consultation that this place was undignified and not a place the Bahá'ís should come. So they went in and rented an exclusive resort place on the reservation at great cost. Then they put up signs to guide the Bahá'ís to this place. No one consulted Billy. Billy and I did not know the plan was changed until we arrived at the reservation. When Billy saw what they had done tears came to his eyes and he told me that no Indians would ever come to this place. He and I drove over to the place he had arranged and most of the Indians were there playing and sitting around talking. The Bahá'ís had the very nice exclusive place, and it was exclusive. If only we would just do as Bahá'u'lláh said and carefully listen. Even in our consultation we seldom really listen or carefully listen to what others are saying. We are usually too filled with our own ideas and thoughts to pay attention to what someone else may be saying.

CHAPTER 19

O GOD! GIVE ME WISDOM

I know that I don't have wisdom and I pray everyday, "O God give me enough wisdom just to know when to shut up." If I had just that wisdom I would be very happy. In fact I think that kind of wisdom can only come through inspiration and a real sensitivity to the feeling of others.

'Abdu'l-Bahá

Instruction :

> *"Beware lest ye harm any soul, or make any heart to sorrow; lest ye wound any man with your words,"*
>
> *SAB-73*

A Bahá'í in Alaska who had a full time job and not much time off decided that he wanted to join the teaching team. So he saved his money and his vacation time for two years. Then he took the first 9 days of his vacation and went to one of those special heavenly banquets the nine day institute.

When he joined the team we were leaving on the Alaska Ferry from Haines on one of those rare beautiful clear days in the middle of summer. The sky was blue and the sea was a deep azure blue. The brilliant green fir trees marched up each side of the hills on both sides of the ferry and the blue tinged glaciers could be seen in the hill sides and the snow-topped peaks glistened in the sunshine. The sea was as calm as a mill pond with only a warm summer breeze generated by the movement of the ferry. Unless one has had the experience of one of these days in Southeast Alaska he cannot possibly grasp the awesome beauty of it.

So started this man's vacation on the teaching team. He was standing next to a Tlingt Indian Bahá'í woman from the Yukon Territory of Canada. Now this woman was a very special and wonderful angel of Bahá'u'lláh. She had been on the team now for almost 2 years. She had rheumatoid arthritis and her neck and shoulders were swollen and extremely painful all the time. She had left her children and husband with their loving support they held down the home front. Every day she taught the Cause of God. She was extremely kind and loving and never complained. She truly lived by the words of:

'Abdu'l-Bahá

Instruction :

> *"Be thoughtful concerning your own spiritual developments and close your eyes to the short comings of one another."*

BWF-365

She had endured all the rigors and hardships. Sleeping in way below freezing weather in unheated log cabins. Using out houses. Taking sponge baths and being away from her children and husband. Still, every day, in spite of her severe pain she gave out with a spirit of love and happiness that touched many hearts and confirmed them in the Cause.

As the ferry ran smoothly across this inside passage this man turned to the Bahá'í woman and exulted, "Isn't this a wonderful vacation."

I found her back in a dark corner of the ferry sobbing her precious heart out and when I asked her what was the matter she sobbed, "Jenabe people think I am on a vacation."

'Abdu'l-Bahá

Instruction :

> *"Beware, beware, lest ye offend the feelings of another."*

SAB-73

Now we all know that the teachings say we must never be offended and we must never offend any heart and no heart must be hurt. Saying this and applying it to your life is two very different things. I know I don't have that kind of wisdom and that is why I pray for it every day. You can see how innocent this Bahá'í teacher was and you can also understand the feelings of the woman, that is after the fact. O God, Please, I beg you to protect me from myself and my lack of wisdom.

CHAPTER 20

MY CALAMITY IS MY PROVIDENCE

When I was in Quebec doing mass teaching with about 35 or 40 Bahá'ís and we were out in the park I was very animatedly giving a fireside. All of a sudden all my thoughts and ideas that usually flow in a torrent were gone. In fact I lost my thoughts right in mid- sentence. The same thing happened to all the other teachers in the park. All at the same time. I learned that evening that at that exact moment one of the Bahá'ís on the team could not take the ragging from one of the people he was trying to teach and he punched him in the nose and knocked his contact down. That was the end of the teaching in that town and it took several days of prayer and consultation with the team before they again became effective.

This has happened even when people just get angry and don't even say anything. On the other hand if the enemies of the Cause rise up against us and there is no truth at all in their accusations, it always works to the benefit of the Faith.

Bahá'u'lláh

Instruction :

> *"O SON OF MAN!*
> *My calamity is My providence, outwardly it*
> *is fire and vengeance, but inwardly it is*
> *light and mercy."*

AHW #51

We had 38 people on the team and a number of local Bahá'ís when we landed in Sitka. The majority were youth between 19 and 25 years old. That first day we enrolled 109 young people between the ages of 13 and 19. So we started some intensive consolidation classes. Sitka has a boarding school and some of these young people came from every corner of Alaska. The rest lived in Sitka.

We were living in the Alaska Native Service hall. The women and girls slept on the balcony on one side and the men slept on the balcony on the other side. We had a number of responsible adults with us also. Now any night you would come to the hall it would appear to be chaos and confusion. Kids everywhere. It was organized confusion. Some of the youth were in one corner learning Bahá'í songs and playing the guitars. In another corner they were learning Indian and Eskimo dances. Others were in the prayer room saying prayers with the prayer watch. Others were sitting with the teachers studying prayers and The Hidden Words and all of them were being deepened in the Love of Bahá'u'lláh. Any stranger that came in would have a hard time trying to figure out what was going on.

Because these children would stay until 10 or 11 p.m. someone in Sitka started a rumor that we were into a sexual orgy with these young people. These were bald-faced lies as the Bahá'ís were angels. They were sacrificing their sleep at night and teaching all day. No one could find any fault with them. One and all they were radiantly beautiful and filled with the spirit of the love of mankind and Bahá'u'lláh.

I knew something was up because some of these kids would phone in and tell me they couldn't come any more as their daddies or mommies said that they were doing bad things at the hall. They tried to tell their parents that all they were doing was learning about God, but the parents wouldn't listen. Also unknown to us some of the parents started calling the police and demanding that they go over to the Bahá'í hall and protect these children.

The police decided to have a raid. Now like I said any night if anyone came in they would not be able to sort out what was going on. However the police chose the night of the Ascension of 'Abdu'l-Bahá and they picked 1 A.M. in the morning. That night we planned to have a round of prayers to commemorate the passing of our beloved Master and every one was in their seats at 5 minutes to one. The seats were placed in a circle. At exactly one O'clock I stood up and began, "He is the all glorious, O God, my God," the door flew open and in came the police. Most of the Bahá'ís did not even look up. They thought it was someone coming in late for prayers. I was facing the door and when I saw all the police rush in, then the whole thing came together in my mind. I just went right on with the prayer and as we had just started you could have heard a pin drop. In fact because we had just started no one was fidgeting in their chairs yet. The Chief of Police put up his hand and stopped the other policemen. They had come in so fast that it carried some of them right up to the chairs. The Chief of Police and the others all listened for several minutes. Then the Chief motioned for all his policemen to follow him. They tip-toed out the door and he even turned the door knob so it wouldn't click.

The next day when the young people came to the hall after school a number of them told me that their parents had called the police the night before. The police told all the parents and anyone else that called. "The best place in Sitka for your children if they are still out so late, is over at that Baha'í hall. You know what they are doing at 1 A.M. in the morning? They are saying prayers. If your children are on the streets of Sitka at 1 A.M. in the morning, believe me they are not saying prayers. We are picking them up all the time. You send your kids over there as it is the best place in Sitka for them if they stay out at night."

Bahá'u'lláh

Instruction :

> *"Nothing save that which profiteth them can befall My loved ones."*

ADJ-69

So you see Bahá'u'lláh is able to turn their lies and slander into victories for His Cause, but let there be just a tiny bit of truth in what they are saying about us, we are finished in that town.

A whole sequence of things took place in Fort Yukon that backs up this principal. This was the start of Massive Encounter planned by the National Spiritual Assembly of Alaska. There were over 30 foot soldiers, a navy made up of two canoes and a river boat and an air force made up of two cesna-180's and a piper cup and we set out to spiritually conquer Alaska.

The air force loaded down their planes with tents and camping equipment and went in ahead of the team. In an open field they put up their tents, dug latrines, and got things ready. The rest of us came in, in a chartered C-46 which had no rear door and the wings actually flapped in the wind. We had just all together completed the Spiritual Transformation classes and it was one soul in many bodies.

We had pregnant women, crippled people, youth, old people and we even had one blind Bahá'í with us. The faces were beaming with light and these warriors of Bahá'u'lláh went from the airport over to tent city singing. The young people helping the old, crippled and the blind man. It was indeed the war of Armageddon.

The city of Fort Yukon was immediately set on fire. Some people responded with fear and consternation and others responded with joy and happiness.

One of our Bahá'ís owned a log cabin in Fort Yukon and we used this for a command post. I went directly to this cabin and a runner came from tent city shouting, "Jenabe come quick, there is a man with a knife in tent city."

I ran over there and sure enough there was a young man with a knife in his hand waving it around and shouting, "Our Bishop said you people come from hell and you came here to take us to hell. Well you are not going to take anyone from Fort Yukon to hell because I am going to cut up your tents and you will have to leave." As I rushed up to him he shouted, "I'll kill you. I'll kill you."

I calmly told him not to make the same mistake the people made when Christ came the first time. Then I said let's have a prayer. Why did I say that? Because the instructions said, "Prayer is your protection and preservation from tests." That was the only reason. This young man said, I'm not going to pray to your 100,000 gods, my bishop said you pray to 100,000 gods.

I said, "Son there is only one God and all prayers go to the same place." I opened up the prayer book and began to read. I didn't know it but this boy's mother had taught him that when someone says a prayer you bow your head, fold your hands and show respect. So he quickly folded up his knife, put it in his pocket, folded his hands, closed his eyes and showed respect.

He had expected us to fight with him, gang up on him, call the police etc. but he never expected us to say a prayer and this disarmed him. When I finished the prayer I said, "OK, now you say one." He got down on his knees and I don't know what he prayed as he did it in Athabascan. When he finished there were tears running down his face. I got down along side of him and put my arm around his shoulder and said. "Those prayers went to the same place now didn't they.

He nodded his head and replied, "Yeah, they went to the same place." I took him up to the cabin gave him some coffee and he sat and played the guitar for a while and then went home and that was the end of the knife attack.

A few days later I was called into Anchorage to meet with the National Spiritual Assembly and I left a very self effacing young man in charge of the team. That night 3 or 4 bully boys came into the hall, shaking their fists, shouting and cursing. They bellowed, "Our Bishop said you people came from the devil and are here to take our people to hell. Now you get out of here. Go pack your gear, get in your airplanes and fly out or we will pour you into your airplanes and you will fly out. We don't want you here."

Now the team had been taught not to interfere if any problems came up. They were told to let the one in charge handle it and everyone else pray. You can't have 38 people solve the problems. So this young team captain went up to this huge man and said very gently and sweetly, "Excuse me mister."

The bully boy took one look at who was talking and didn't pay any more attention to him. He was probably looking for me. The team members all began to sing very softly the remover of difficulties while the team captain persisted in trying to talk to the man. Finally these men realized no one was listening to them and they shut up. The leader listened to the song. Then very dramatically he shook his fist at the ceiling and shouted, "O God where are you, where are you!" and he ran out the door with his buddies right behind him.

About a week later our National Spiritual Assembly Secretary got a phone call from the Native Hospital and it was this same leader of the gang that was going to chase us out of Fort Yukon. He said, "I am in the hospital in Anchorage and I don't know anyone and I thought maybe the Bahá'ís could visit me."

This Bishop had been serving the Indians and Eskimos of Alaska for thirty years and he was quite famous, known as the Flying Bishop of Alaska as he made his rounds for births, baptisms, weddings and funerals across the north land flying his own airplane.

His next move was to send some spies over to our camp and find out what our plans were. This, of course, was very easy as we had no secrets and we did not need spies as our Supreme Commander is Bahá'u'lláh and He is directing this dramatic engagement from His Retreats of Glory. So he found out we were going to send five teachers into a small village and so the Bishop flew in ahead of us. He called all the people together and warned them, "The monster referred to in the Bible that in the last days is to come up out of the bottomless pit and devour the children is Bahá'ís and they are coming to your village." The people of the village were appalled. They asked this Bishop if he meant that the Bahá'ís were coming to eat their children. His response was, well that is what the Bible said would happen and these Bahá'ís were definitely that monster.

The people said, "Well no one is going to eat our children, we will kill the Bahá'ís first." The Bishop further advised them that if they had to do this then all the men in the village should participate as the police would not arrest everybody in the village. The Bishop then got into his plane and flew away.

I had no idea of what went on, as stated above we had no spies and relied on Bahá'u'lláh only. The three airplanes landed and unloaded the five friends and their supplies and took off again, leaving the Bahá'ís on the runway with their things. A cabin had been arranged for them to stay in. It was rectangular in shape with only one door and the windows were small and right up next to the roof. Windows were often made that way in order to be above the snow drifts in the winter. I had been with the scouting team when we rented the cabin so I knew the layout. Across the entryway where the door was, instead of a porch they had a large table with built on benches on both sides so that people coming in could sit down and take off their boots before going into the cabin proper and also this table with attached seats could be used for eating. There was just enough room at the end of the table to enter the rest of the cabin.

The five angels of Bahá'u'lláh had just moved their supplies and equipment up from the airfield to the cabin and all were busy getting things put away. The door flew open and on the door side of the table all the men and boys crowded in. They had in their hands' guns, knives, clubs and broken bottles.

Their leader announced, "Our Bishop has told us that you people are the monsters referred to in the Bible and that you have come up out of the bottomless pit to eat our children. No one is going to eat our children because no one is going to leave here alive. We are going to kill you."

The team captain in charge of this team was the same one that was crying on the ferry about the vacation mentioned above. She being a native herself knew that the courtesy of their country was to have a cup of coffee before you did anything else. Whenever a friend, stranger or anyone came in they were first given a cup of coffee, then they sat and talked about their business or whatever. So she walked right up and faced this leader off across the table and said, "Would you mind if we had our coffee first?"

"Go ahead and have your coffee, but no one is leaving here alive anyway,"

So the gas stove was pumped up and the coffee was started. "Would you mind if we had prayers while we are waiting for the coffee to boil?" the team captain asked.

"Go ahead," he said, "I think anyone who eats children should say prayers."

These five Bahá'ís sat opposite the men of the village and they said Tablets of Ahmad, and prayers for protection etc. The villagers bowed their heads and listened. When the coffee was ready, the team captain poured a styro-foam cup and took it over and gave it to the leader of the villagers. He took his gun and put it in the corner and then sat down on the bench and put cream and sugar in his coffee. The other team members gave coffee to the rest of the men and they one and all put their guns, clubs, knives and broken bottles in the corner. Those that could sat down and the others stood behind. The Bahá'ís all got coffee for themselves and sat down facing the villagers across the table. Now, of course, custom must be followed, that is you talk as you drink your coffee.

"You people are really nice people," said the leader. "How is it possible that you eat children."

The team leader responded, "What nonsense, I have children myself. The monster that comes up out of the bottomless pit and devours the children is the alcohol, drugs and lack of morals. We would not ever even dream of hurting children. The reason we have come here is to try to save our native children." This was followed by a very intense fireside and this Bishop had gotten all the men to the fireside for us and many of the men became Bahá'ís and some of them brought their wives and women folk to become Bahá'ís also.

This Bishop didn't give up, he then found out that the whole team was moving to a small town. This is a small town on the Anchorage-Fairbanks highway. They had seven churches in this town. The Bishop went to the town and visited the preachers and priests and called a special meeting. For the first time in the history of the place all the churches came together. The Bishop warned the people that the Bahá'ís were coming and he further warned them that the Bahá'ís would hypnotize the people if you even looked in their eyes and they put something in the coffee to make people become Bahá'ís and he told them that this is what happened in the village before.

These men of the churches called special meetings and warned their congregations. The people were terrified. When our car caravan arrived, parents went out collecting their children and closed and locked their doors. The streets were instantly deserted. The Bahá'ís did not know what was going on so they doubled up on their prayers.

Some of the youth of the town talked between themselves and decided that they would meet the Bahá'ís and they would not drink their coffee nor look into their eyes. It was hilarious to see these young men looking down and trying to avoid eye contact and the unsuspecting Bahá'ís trying to make eye contact. In any event some of these youth became Bahá'ís. Then they went through the town telling everyone

that they did not drink coffee or look into the Bahá'ís eyes
and they still became Bahá'ís, because what these Bahá'ís
said made sense and for no other reason. So the town opened
up. We were there for about two weeks and the churches lost
their followers. The people of the town were honest and fair-
minded people and they refused to sanction such nonsense.

Bahá'u'lláh

Instruction :

*". . . such things as throw consternation
into the hearts of all men come to pass only
that each soul may be tested by the
touchstone of God."*

KI-52

The last thing the Bishop tried was a complete turn
around. He went to the lower 48 states and recruited some
youth to work for him during the next summer vacations
from their universities. He took them to a retreat for training
and he used our exact schedule, even dawn prayers, individual
prayers and study time.

'Abdu'l-Bahá

Instruction :

*"Investigate and study the Holy Scriptures
word by word so that you may attain
knowledge of the mysteries hidden therein.
Be not satisfied with words, but seek to
understand the spiritual meanings hidden in
the heart of words. . ."*

DAL-40

The only difference was instead of using the Hidden
Words as we do, he used the bible. But they still studied it

"word by word looking for the spiritual meanings that lie hidden in the heart of words."

Then he took this group of 15 youth up to Alaska and rented a big house for them. Which was in a town on our next summer's schedule. He told them that their job for the summer was to so love the Bahá'ís that they would all become Christians. It was to be a war of Bahá'í love versus Christian love.

Our team was met at the airport and invited to come share their house with them. The team following the instructions of responding to invitations were delighted to do so. They moved into this luxury house and these young Christian youth were wonderful and loving and from their careful study of the words of Jesus were truly God loving Christians. They soon discovered that questions they were unable to resolve during their study Bahá'u'lláh very clearly explained to their complete satisfaction. They explained that because they were working for the Bishop they could not accept the Faith then but they promised after the job finished and they returned to their schools they would become Bahá'ís.

CHAPTER 21

WITH FIRE WE TEST THE GOLD

Follow the instructions and Bahá'u'lláh will turn this opposition into victory as these cases clearly show. We still must be tested. These tests sometimes are quite severe but they can also bring victories to the Cause of God.

Bahá'u'lláh

Instruction :

"Do men think when they say 'We believe' they shall be let alone and not be put to proof;"

KI 8-9

In South Carolina we had a new Bahá'í join the teaching team. Her name was Brenda and she became a Bahá'í during the mass teaching and she went through our institute at Frogmore. Then she gave herself to Bahá'u'lláh. Brenda was a little woman 19 years old. She was small and thin and what she lacked in physical stature she made up for in the spiritual. She was so bright and beautiful and self sacrificing and she glowed with that divine brightness.

The first day out she radiated love and was successful in finding some new Bahá'ís. Also on her first day a man put his dog on her and it tore out the back of her leg. She was taken to the hospital and the doctor gave her a tetanus shot and sewed up the back of her leg with many stitches. When she came in that night, she never once complained or found fault with the man that had put the dog on her. She

only talked about all the wonderful people she met that day
and the wonderful new Bahá'ís she had found.

I told her that tomorrow she should stay in, stay off of
her leg, rest and recover. She said, "Please don't keep me
in as I must tell the people about Bahá'u'lláh." So I let her
go out.

The second day out half of the people she met became
Bahá'ís and Brenda was even more loving and beautiful.
That evening I noticed that she had on a short sleeve blouse.
Her arm looked red below the sleeve line so Ilifted the sleeve
and her arm from her shoulder to her elbow was all swollen
up and angry red from the shot. I also noticed that Brenda
was limping very badly. So again I told her that now she
must stay in and get off of her feet and let her arm and leg
heal properly. Brenda began to cry and expostulated, "Jenabe,
if I don't go out tomorrow the people that I would have met
and given the message will never know because all the
teachers are all teaching someone else. "Please, please," She
begged through her tears. So once again I gave in and out
she went.

The third day, everyone she met with no exceptions
became Bahá'ís. One can see through this again that this
Cause is indeed built on sacrifice. That night her team
captain came to me and told me that Brenda had fainted on
the street. So I went to her and asked her if it was because
of her arm and leg. She told me that she was anemic and
she could not function on the light breakfast, apple or orange
we had for lunch and a good dinner. Now I was upset with
her and told her that every member of the team is always
asked if they have any medical problems and when we asked
her she said she had none. We can deal with these problems
when and if we know they exist. So this time I did not relent
even with her crying. I insisted that she stay in and I
informed the cook to see that she had a good lunch every

day in order to help her get her strength back. As I left her I saw the prayer list for the day and sure enough Brenda was scheduled for prayers at 1 A.M.. So I crossed her name off the list and informed her that she was not to get up for prayers, I wanted her on complete rest and I wanted her fully recovered. So Brenda cried some more over her prayers being cancelled.

At about 3 A.M., Brenda told me, she could not sleep. If she lay on her right side the pain in her leg was excruciating and if she lay on her left side the pain in her arm was unbearable and if she lay on her back both her leg and her arm caused severe pain. So she decided that even if I got angry, she had to go talk to Bahá'u'lláh. She got out of bed and went to the kitchen of the house we were in where the prayer watch was going on and sat down with the others praying.

'Abdu'l-Bahá

Instruction :

"If others hurl their darts against you, offer them milk and honey in return; if they poison your lives, sweeten their souls;"

SAB-24

The outside kitchen door opened and in came two very big men. They started right in being loud and vulgar and they began to make obscene remarks to the girls. Now we had told the people in the neighborhood that they could come over anytime day or night to learn about Bahá'í. The instructions are that if they say war, we say peace and if they say hate we show forth and say love. These blessed souls on this prayer watch tried very hard to do this and as conflict and contention are absolutely forbidden by Bahá'u'lláh, they went right on with their prayers.

3

Bahá'u'lláh

Instruction :

*"Conflict and contention are categorically
forbidden in His Book. This is a decree of
God in this Most Great Revelation."*

TB-221

Except for Brenda, who got angry and told herself, "I
need to talk to Bahá'u'lláh and these jokers are ruining my
prayers. If they don't stop and shut up I will get up and pitch
them out on their ears." Now Brenda would have been lucky
to weigh in at 90 pounds with her clothes on and soaking
wet. These two men each weighed about 220 pounds. Then
it hit Brenda as to what she was doing. "My God! Didn't
I learn anything at that institute? Didn't `Abdu'l-Bahá say,
'If they poison your lives sweeten their souls?' Here I am
wanting to kill these guys. O Bahá'u'lláh please forgive me."
As it was her turn to pray she opened her book to the prayers
for forgiveness. Now when this sweet angelic child turned
to the Blessed Beauty asking His forgiveness she opened up
the doors to heaven and the concourse on high and the
unseen angels rank upon rank and file upon file descended
on that house and into that kitchen. One of the men that had
come in jumped up and went out the door so fast that he
almost tore the door from its hinges. The other man told us
later that when Brenda started to pray he also wanted to go
with his friend, but he could not. He was paralysed, frozen
in his chair. He said he could not even blink his eyes. Now
it was very quite and the prayers went on. When it was
Brenda's turn to pray again this man got his voice back and
he said he wanted to explain and he was truly sorry for what
he had done in coming over.

Today in the hospital the doctors had told him and his
wife that their baby son could not live through the night that

it would surely die before morning and there was nothing they could do about it. His wife had stayed in the hospital with the baby, but he could not stay and watch his son die. He loved that little boy so very much. He had gone home and his friend had come over to help him and his friend had tried everything to help him get his mind off of his boy, nothing worked. In desperation his friend had suggested that they go over where the Bahá'ís were staying and pick a fight and as they would have to defend themselves, he could get his mind off the baby. As he was hurt and angry over his loss he had agreed and was truly sorry.

Brenda said, "Please everybody let's say healing prayers for his baby." With saying this, she said the long healing prayer and all the others on the prayer watch also said healing prayers. When the last healing prayer was said, Bernardo jumped out of his chair, straight up in the air and came down with a crash and he shouted, "I don't know who you people are and I don't know where you people come from, but I know you are from God! I know you are from God! I have been running away from You all my life, God, and now you caught me, now you caught me. I'm not running any more. I'm yours. I'm yours." He then got down on his knees and with tears running down his face, confessed all his sins from the day he was born. Now with all the shouting and banging in the kitchen everyone in the house woke up and it sounded like a wild preacher in the kitchen. All the Bahá'ís in the house started singing the Remover of Difficulties which further increased the spiritual power being generated. Bernardo signed his enrollment card and said his running away from God cost him the life of his child. He went home.

In the morning just as we were getting in the cars to go teaching, Bernardo comes running up shouting, "Wait for me! Wait for me! I am going with you. A miracle, my son is alive and the doctors don't understand. At about 3 A.M.

this morning the child started to recover and the doctors say this is impossible, but I know because I was here last night. I am going with you."

Bernardo joined the team and became a wonderful teacher. Just follow the instructions and if they poison your life you sweeten their souls.

A large group of Bahá'ís came to Mexico for teacher training and after the Institute I took this team out for what we call field training. Which means trying to apply what we learn in the class to real life with real people. We went to a village I had been into several times and we only had one Bahá'í family in the village and everyone else showed no interest at all. Again I did not follow the proper procedure of going first to do a good proclamation with the authorities and tell them first what we planned to do. We just went to the park and I turned on the amplifier and using the microphone invited the people to come hear about Bahá'í. The only ones that came were a lot of children and the police. The police arrested me and took me off to the police station for disturbing the peace. The children then scattered through the village and told everyone that a man was in the park talking about a new message from God and the police put him in jail. The Bahá'ís on the team prayed. When the chief of police came I had a very wonderful fireside with all the policemen and they advised me to go ahead as they felt Bahá'í was exactly what their village needed. So when I left the Jail the villagers all came to me to express their concern and so we ended with a great proclamation and some great teaching and firesides. We were able to reach and teach everyone because of being arrested.

CHAPTER 22

THE POWER OF PRAYER

The power of prayer can't be over emphasized. From the above-mentioned knife attack to getting arrested, there is always prayer.

'Abdu'l-Bahá

Instruction :

"Besides all this, prayer and fasting is the cause of awakening and mindfulness and is conducive to protection and preservation from tests."

DAL-27

I was in a village in Mexico and their were 12 to 15 people in the room. Most of them were Bahá'ís. One man sitting opposite of me began asking questions about Bahá'u'lláh and Bahá'í. He seemed satisfied with the answers so I extended to him the loving invitation to join and help us.

He responded, "You know accepting a new religion isn't like jumping into a bath. I know a lot of my friends become Bahá'ís the minute they hear about it, but not me. I'm going to study about Bahá'í and it will probably take years. When I am sure that Bahá'u'lláh is from God, then I will become a Bahá'í."

I told him that was wonderful as a basic Bahá'í principal is individual investigation of the truth and to please take all the time he needed. In the meantime a young man that was behind me pulled on my shirt sleeve and said, "Mister can I please be a Bahá'í, my friends are all Bahá'ís and during our siesta time we read Bahá'í prayers and I love Bahá'í very much. Can I please be a Bahá'í."

"Of course you can be a Bahá'í," I said. I got out a prayer book and began to explain about the obligatory prayer. The young man with the bright eyes that had been asking all the questions, saw that I was showing the new Bahá'í something, he said, "What's that?

I answered, "It's a prayer book."

"May I see it?" he enquired.

"Of course," I said and passed the book over to him and took out of my bag another one and went on about the obligatory prayer. I heard a deep sigh from across the room and looked up. Bright eyes had tears on his cheeks and he said. "Man I studied enough, I know this is from God! I know this is from God! I am ready to be a Bahá'í.

Bahá'u'lláh

Instruction :

> *"And when he determineth to leave his home, for the sake of the Cause of His Lord, let him put his whole trust in God, as the best provision for his journey, and array himself with the robe of virtue."*

TDP 5-6

Another most wonderful experience happened to a young couple that I stayed with when I was in Nigeria. It is about prayer and obedience.

The young man had just gotten his degree in education and him and his lovely young wife had just been married. They sat down and wrote to the International Goals Committee in the United States explaining that the goal of their lives was to pioneer and now that he had his degree they were willing to go to any goal that might need pioneers where he could work. This goals committee wrote back and informed them that as they were young and had no experience, it would be better if they waited a few years. So this young man applied for work and was accepted in a town in the United States. They had an old car, they got a lease on an efficiency apartment, made down payments on furniture and signed a contract for the next school year.

For their honeymoon they had agreed to save their money and go on pilgrimage. They received their invitation to go to Haifa and it was right before his work started. So they were off to New York driving their old car. They parked their car at the airport and flew off to heaven.

One evening this young man mentioned to one of the members of the Universal House of Justice about wanting to pioneer. The next day this House member looked up the couple and asked them, if they would like to go to Africa. Of course they would like to go to Africa and they said that after he finished his school contract next year they would make plans to go. The member of the House of Justice explained that because of the Biafra war going on in Nigeria, the pioneers had left and they needed someone to go right away, would they consider this.

They went up to the shrine of the Báb and prayed and then went down to the airline office and traded in their return ticket to New York for a one way ticked to Logos, Nigeria. They wrote and sent their parking ticket to the Bahá'ís of New York to get their old car and sell it. They wrote the Bahá'ís in the town they had just moved into and asked them to sub-let their apartment. They wrote the school board of the town that had hired him and said they were sorry, but couldn't make his first job.

On the airplane flying out over the Sahara Desert, their conversation went something like this.

Him, "What language do they speak in Nigeria?"

Her, "I don't know. Do we need a visa?"

Him, "I don't know. Where will we go when we land?"

Her, "I don't know. How will we get from the airport?"

Him, "I don't know. What are we going to do?"

Her, "I don't know what your going to do, but I'm going to pray." With that she got out her prayer book and started saying the Tablet of Aḥmad. The husband also got out his prayer book. When his wife finished he started. She said a Tablet of Aḥmad and he said a Tablet of Aḥmad. She said another and he said another and so the miles went by.

A man came down the isle of the airplane and stopped by their seat. "Where are you going?" he asked.

"We're going to Logos, Nigeria.?" the husband replied.

"What are you going to do there?" the man asked again.

"I'm going to try to find work if I can.?" he said.

"What kind of work are you looking for?"

"I'm a school teacher."

"Thank God I found you," exulted the man. "I have the largest American School in west Africa and because of this Biafra mess I need teachers. I have been up in England trying to find teachers and not very successfully. Do you want a job?"

With that he pulled a contract out of his pocket and handed it to the husband.

The husband was over joyed and signed the contract without reading it. The salary was more than double what he had been offered in America. The man then turned to the young wife and asked her what she liked to do. She explained that she did not have a degree as she had only finished high school, but she liked art. The man took out another contract and gave it to the wife and said, "OK you work in the art department." Then the man told them that English was the common language. When they asked about visas he took out work visas already filled in by the government and all they had to do was fill in the spaces with their names and passport numbers.

The man also told them he would take care of them at the airport in Logos. A limo was waiting and the owner of the school whisked them off to an apartment house and gave them the keys to a fully furnished two bedroom apartment. He then took them out to the garage and gave them the keys to a new car explaining that all this came with the job. Everything they gave up was given back to them even before they arrived at their pioneering post.

CHAPTER 23

DON'T BE IN A HURRY

Bahá'u'lláh

Instruction :

"Make me as a lamp shining throughout Thy lands that those in whose hearts the light of Thy knowledge gloweth and the yearning for Thy love lingereth may be guided by its radiance."

TB-152

We spend hours and hours in prayer asking Bahá'u'lláh to send us those hearts He has prepared and to send us to them. Which He does, then right at that point we are doing something else and the opportunity is lost.

In the Aleutian Islands I had a friend who was a school teacher on the Island and his wife. We had a number of firesides and this couple seemed very interested. As I was starting up a King Crab operation, this friend and I would put on 3/4" wet suits and using scuba gear we would swim in the frozen waters of the Bering Sea checking out this King Crab resource. For me it was business and for my teacher friend it was R&R (Rest and Recreation).

One day as I was going somewhere in a hurry past my friends house he called me and asked me in to answer some very important questions about Bahá'u'lláh and Bahá'í. I told him that I was in a hurry and would talk to him later, and off I went. That night I had a night-mare. My friend and I were swimming and he lost his mouth piece and began to sink. I swam down and got him by the hair and was struggling with might and mane to get him to the surface. I lost my hold and I watched him slowly descend into an ice cold watery grave. The next morning as soon as I could I rushed off to his house and said I was ready to answer all his questions. He told me that he had second thoughts and was no longer at all interested in Bahá'í and did not wish to hear any more about it.

In Western Washington State there was a Local Spiritual Assembly and they were down to 8 members and so on the first of April they started having several hours of prayer every Wednesday and on the second evening they were all in one of the friend's houses. Their prayers were very intense and the eight people were in that wonderful heavenly delight brought on by their sincere desire and yearning after God. The door bell rang and the owner of the house, very upset at the interruption of such a heavenly repast, answered the door.

"Is this the house where I can learn about Bahá'í," asked the visitor.

"Yes it is," replied the host. "We are having a special prayer meeting right now and would you like to come back another time please?" He closed the door in the seeker's face and returned to his prayers. When it was discovered what had happened the other friends were a little upset. Fortunately Bahá'u'lláh wanted that heart so he sent him back and the Local Assembly was formed.

'Abdu'l-Bahá

Instruction :

> *At this time and at this period we must avail ourselves of this most great opportunity. We must not sit inactive for one*

> *moment; we must sever ourselves from composure, rest, tranquility, goods, property, life and attachment to material things."*
>
> *QM-13*

In the Philippines we had about 150 full time teachers and we were doing a 24-hour prayer watch and having dawn prayers every morning and all the teachers were either teaching or praying. One afternoon we had a large number of contacts and the teachers actually set up a production line for enrollments. The teacher would take the contact through the teaching book and answer the seeker's questions. Another teacher would then help this new Bahá'í to fill out the enrollment card. The new Bahá'í was then given a teaching book and was told to go at once and teach with another teacher as his coach in case the new Bahá'í could not answer all the questions. As we know if you want to really be confirmed in the Cause of God, then teach the Cause of God. This process was accelerating with more and more people becoming Bahá'ís and new Bahá'ís were busily teaching new Bahá'ís. This is the true meaning of Mass Teaching and one could see the process evolving into "Entry by Troops."

Some of the team members, after checking the time, gathered up all the team members because it was dinner time. They stopped the teaching to go to dinner.

Never, never stop teaching for any excuse. Dinner can wait, sleeping can wait and transportation can even wait. You may have to sleep over on someone's floor but so what. Isn't our sole aim and purpose to rescue a sick and disillusioned humanity from the slough of heedlessness and materialism and bring them all safely aboard Bahá'u'lláh's Crimson Ark?

Universal House of Justice

Instruction :

*"Upon our efforts depends in very large
measure the fate of humanity."*

WG-120

The way to do it, and we should keep this in mind, was done in Canada on the Quebec project. One of our full time teachers was a member of the National Spiritual Assembly. He stopped at an intercontinental bus stop and struck up a conversation with a truly very interested person. When it was time for the bus to leave and as the teacher was just getting started, he bought a ticket and got on the bus for about a 4-hour bus trip. He enrolled this person on the bus and then on the way back he enrolled another person.

All the teaching work that is successful comes from following the instructions and from experience I can say that about 98 percent of our problems are caused by not following the instructions. Most of our tests in life, when we will be truthful with ourselves, are self inflicted. Just look at the problems in the world today and the root cause is by our disobedience to Bahá'u'lláh.

CHAPTER 24

SOY BAHÁ'Í

This is also true of our individual tests for the most part. However Bahá'u'lláh does send us some very severe tests and sometimes they seem to be more than the human heart can withstand.

'Abdu'l-Bahá

Instruction :

"Thou didst write of afflictive tests that assailed thee. To the loyal soul, a test is but God's grace and favour;"

SAB-181

In Mexico there is a small village called Ixtapexi, in the state of Oaxaca. This village has been continuously inhabited for as far back as men can remember. Ixtapexi is on top of a ridge and one can look down into the valley below from three sides. The water comes down a hill from the 4th side and sometime in the far distant past the Indians had cut into the rock a canal right down the center of the ridge. The houses were then built on each side of the canal. All the people had to do was to step out of their houses and get the clean fresh mountain water out of the canal. This water was then sent down the mountain on the three sides to water the fruit trees. Apple trees, peach trees and pear trees grew in the high sierras of Ixtapexi. Also between the houses the tall dark green fir trees grew and the people had planted the bougainvillea flowers alongside the fir trees. These plants then climbed up the fir trees and great cascades of red, white,

purple, orange and pink bougainvillea flowers burst forth
from their branches.

There was a radiant beauty about Ixtapexi, with its
flowering fir trees, clean cold mountain air and water, setting
like a little jewel in the fresh air of the high sierras. When
the Spaniards came and invaded the land, these proud people
fought with a will and determination, but they were no match
for the guns and were killed and enslaved. They were made
to dismantle the temple and forced to reuse the material for
building their Christian church. These fellows very carefully
put their sacred figures and stones in the wall of the church
so that when they faced the altar and cross they were also
facing their ancient religion and culture. So hundreds of
years ago they already had the vision of progressive revelation.

One can tell that I had a special love for Ixtapexi. As
there was no road up to the village I had to park my truck
down below and walk up through the fruit orchards to the
top. There was one more most beautiful thing in Ixtapexi.
This was a baby girl. When I first met her she was about
18 months old and as her mother was a Bahá'í I would hold
the baby and say prayers for her. Before she was two years
old she already knew all the Bahá'í songs and children's
prayers. She even knew the short obligatory prayer by heart.
She would watch the road and when she spotted my truck
coming she would dash into the house and shout, "Mama!
Mama! my tio (uncle) is coming. My uncle is coming." Then
run as fast as her tiny legs would allow down the mountain
and throw herself into my arms, hug me around the neck,
put her head into the hollow of my neck and say, "O my
tio! O my tio!" and hug and squeeze me as I carried her up
the mountain. She would then sing in a voice as pure as the
fresh clean mountain air, "Soy Bahá'í, Soy Bahá'í, Si Amigo
Soy Bahá'í. Porque Yo amo a Bahá'u'lláh. Si Amigo Soy
Bahá'í." She knew all the verses and would sing them to me
as we climbed. Whenever she got to the word Bahá'í or

Bahá'u'lláh, I got a special little hug around my neck. Now down in Santa Domingo Tamaltapec I had 150 children in my children's classes but this little angel way up on top of the high sierras had my heart completely.

Her mother told me that in the two and a half years that I visited this village, her baby had developed a sixth sense. Just about a day or two before I would plan to go to Ixtapexi this baby would stop playing with the other children and would go tell her mother that her tio was coming. Then she would sit and watch the road waiting for me. She was never more than two days off on my arrival at the village. Even after 28 years I can still close my eyes and see this angel flying down the mountain side, her long raven black hair waving in the wind, her little shift of a dress and her big dark eyes filled with excitement and love as she raced to meet me. So dear reader you can see that I had a very special love for a very special person and of all the villages that I have gone to before and since can never compare to the village of Ixtapexi and the pure love I found there.

From the time I first met her and she could walk, she never failed to meet me on the mountain. She was my special angel and my delight and I looked forward to my visits to Ixtapexi with the same excitement that she showed upon my arrival. This time, however, she did not come flying down the mountain and as I came into the village I spotted her mother, Elmira. Her mother was a tall well built woman with a soft and gentle character. When she saw me coming she burst into tears and threw herself into my arms and cried, "Jenabe, my baby died, my baby died."

My heart broke into a thousand pieces and if it had not been for the need of her mother I would have fallen completely apart. I took Elmira over to a bench under one of the trees, held her close and explained through my tears how Bahá'u'lláh is the loving and tender gardener. He looks down and sees our little one living in a dark corner of the garden and in His infinite wisdom, lovingly and tenderly transplants it into a bright and sunny spot in another garden. He knows what is best for each one of His plants and all we know and understand is the one we love so much has been taken from us.

Elmira said, "Jenabe, I know this and I have reconciled myself to this, but when I saw you coming my baby just died all over again. Let me tell you how she died. She had a very high fever and was just burning up. I was holding her in my arms and she touched her head and said, 'Mamma, Mamma my head hurts, my head hurts.' Then she touched her chest and said, ' Mamma, Mamma my chest hurts, my chest hurts.' Then she started rocking in my arms and she sang, 'Soy Bahá'í, Soy Bahá'í. Si Amigo Soy Bahá'í. Porque Yo Amo a Bahá'u'lláh....' and she was gone."

The years have gone by and when I think about her tears still come to my eyes and if I were once again to climb the mountain to Ixtapexi my heart would break and the tears would flow. I know Bahá'u'lláh has said, "I have made death a messenger of joy to thee. Wherefore dost thou grieve?"

Through the years I have come to understand that this is for the one that goes not for those of us left behind. I have seen well-meaning Bahá'ís go to a Bahá'í funeral and smile and beam about how wonderful it is. Please dear friends don't do this. We can take the example of the heart break of the Guardian at the passing of 'Abdu'l-Bahá as an example. Just be most loving and kind and compassionate to these souls who are in the middle of bereavement and be very careful that you don't add to their heartbreak. From personal experience I know the feeling that we go through at these times. One is almost numb with grief and that is with the knowledge that Bahá'u'lláh has given us about death.

This is a good example of the kinds of tests that Providence sends to us that are not of our making. In the above story of the child in Ixtapexi, I thank God with all my heart that he gave me that baby to hold for just a short time and my life is that much richer for the wonderful experience.

CHAPTER 25

HI-JACKING

The only way we can prove our love for Bahá'u'lláh is through tests. To love Him when there is no storm and all is calm sailing is one thing, but to love Him and obey Him when faced with overwhelming storms is then a true love. I pray for tests but I also pray most sincerely to pass the tests. I hate failing the tests when Bahá'u'lláh sends them to me.

'Abdu'l-Bahá

Instruction :

"Besides all this, prayer and fasting is the cause of awakening and mindfulness and conducive to protection and preservation from tests."

BWF-368

A good example of failing tests was the Hijacking. I had just finished a nine-day institute in Panchgani, India and on the last day I came down with a most severe case of malaria. I started my medication and when I got down to Bombay the heat along with the malaria was unbearable. I called Japan Airlines and had my ticket changed to leave on the next flight to Tokyo where I could get out of the heat, get into an air-conditioned hotel and sweat out the attack.

At the airport in Bombay I noticed some Japanese checking in ahead of me. They had on the black pants and white shirts like those worn by flight crews and I wondered at the time why they would be checking in at the ticket counter. After check-in I went into the rest room and these same men were in the rest room putting on their ties, flight crew jackets and caps. Then as we proceeded to the security check these same men went right past security with the other flight crews. Of course they carried their guns, hand grenades and nitro-glycerin in their bags. I was quite ill but I wondered about them when I saw them again in the waiting lounge without their hats, ties and jackets once again.

The plane took off and my seat was next to an Arab from Saudi Arabia. He had on a white robe and little black ring on his head. He introduced himself as Mr. Manshadi. We spoke for a few minutes and because of my illness I lay back in the seat and closed my eyes. As soon as the plane reached its altitude and the seat belt sign was turned off these five men jumped up with guns in their hands and demanded that we all put our heads down, close our eyes and shut up or they would blow our brains out. We all did as we were told and the plane was diverted to Dacca, Bangladesh where it landed and parked at the end of the field.

The temperature started to go up and these hijackers went about their business of terrifying the passengers. They would walk up and down the isle of the airplane and randomly hit people with the butts of their guns, they knew exactly how to do this to cause the blood to flow but not break any heads or bone. Of course one of them came up and side swiped Mr. Manshadi and the blood ran down his face. At this point I realized that Bahá'u'lláh had set me up to be tested. I distinctly remembered 'Abdu'l-Bahá's table talk where he said that if someone came in and attacked him, he would forgive them but if they attacked Siyyid Manshadi he would defend him with his life. This all went through my mind as the blood stained Mr. Manshadi's white robe. Did I jump up and defend Mr. Manshadi? No I surely did not. I sat there and reasoned that if I got up to defend Mr. Manshadi the hijacker would shoot me and go ahead and beat on Mr. Manshadi anyhow. This would be suicide and suicide is forbidden by Bahá'u'lláh. So I just sat there and realized that I had flunked the test.

Then 'Abdu'l-Bahá said if a person has ten bad qualities and one good one look for the one and forget the ten. So I determined to do this and I even said Tablets of Aḥmad to help me. The temperature went up to over 40 degrees C and some of the 154 passengers began to pass out from heat prostration and other ailments and although there were some doctors among the passengers these hijackers would not let them look after the sick and ailing. Where Bahá'u'lláh says to love your enemies and I had been going around and around the world in country after country and even here in Bangladesh telling people to love loveable people is easy but to love the unlovable is difficult but where the real test of loving comes in.

'Abdu'l-Bahá

Instruction :

"The meaning of this is that ye must show forth tenderness and love to every human being, even to your enemies,"

SAB-21

I flunked this test all the way. I didn't love them at all in fact for the five and a half days that I was their prisoner my hate for them grew. If I were to say that I loved them I would in fact be the world's greatest hypocrite. I even remembered the story from "Ten Days in the Light of 'Akká" by `Abdu'l-Bahá page 103, Jesus and his disciples as they walked along and came upon a dead dog. Each disciple as he passed had something bad to say about the dog, it stank, it had maggots on it etc. but when Jesus came he said, "Did you ever see such beautiful white teeth?" So I checked out my hijacker's teeth and they even had ugly yellow or stained teeth. So I flunked the test of finding even one good quality.

My back went out on me, so on top of the malaria I ended up on the floor. The toilets overflowed and the filth ran down the aisle of the airplane. The stench was unbearable. When they sent out food to the plane the hijackers would not serve it until it became uneatable so after the first day most of the passengers quit eating. At night the hijackers put nitro-glycerin around the doors so that if anyone tried to enter the plane the whole plane would be blown up. After the first day and before my back went out I realized that these men would not hesitate to kill all of us. So I determined to try to save some of us any way. So I whispered to Mr. Manshadi, "Look there are 154 of us and only 5 of them lets take them out. Some of us may be killed but the rest will be saved." He agreed but one of the hijackers saw me talking and he came up and said move over there. So we were separated before we had time to make a plan. So with the next two passengers I made the same proposal. They pleaded with me not to do it even though I explained that they would not hesitate to kill us all. They said someone from outside would save us. I responded that why should someone from outside try to save us if we were not willing to save ourselves. Again I was caught talking and moved, and again and again and so on. Of all the people on the plane that I tried to get to help me only Mr. Manshadi had agreed. So I gave it up and flunked another test by trying to foment a rebellion.

The thing was resolved after the five and a half days and I was carried off the airplane on a stretcher and put in the hospital in Dacca. I was the only passenger that had a steady stream of visitors in the hospital. I had done my institutes and a mass teaching project in Bangladesh and had made many friends. They argued that this was Bahá'u'lláh's way of telling me to come and stay in Bangladesh.

'Abdu'l-Bahá

Instruction :

". . .and He hath forbidden them to interfere at all with political problems. He hath even prohibited the believers from discussing political affairs."

BWF-447

In the institutes that I conduct one of the points that I try very hard to make is the one to stay out of politics. If someone asks you a question with political overtones, just quote the writings, never talk right off the top of your head. Now did I follow my own advise? I got a telephone call while I was in the hospital from Reuters International Press. They told me that as I was one of the only Americans on the plane and all of the United States had been praying for me. They then asked me how I felt about the way it had been handled. Right off the top of my head I said, "I think we made a big mistake to pay those monsters five million dollars and let five of their buddies out of jail to do this same thing to other innocent passengers."

Headlines the next day in some of the U.S. newspapers. BAHÁ'Í INTERNATIONAL TEACHER CONDEMNS JAPANESE GOVERNMENT. So I flunked the test of staying out of politics and sticking to the writings. When I returned to Alaska about 100 Bahá'ís were at the airport and so was the TV people and as I came off the plane all the Alaskan Bahá'ís sang "I love you and you love me." They had also had TV coverage while I was on the plane and they had told the press that I was a lover and would probably love the hijackers off the plane. With the international TV running did I give the message, did I explain about the wolves and the sheep as `Abdu'l-Bahá explains it in Some Answered Questions? With the eye of the world on me all I said was catch those monsters and kill them. So again I flunked the test and blew away amarvelous opportunity to help proclaim the message of God. Like I said I hate to flunk tests and I know that one day I must take the test over so I pray daily for Bahá'u'lláh's protection when it happens.

CHAPTER 26

JAMAL EFFENDI

Bahá'u'lláh

Instruction :

"Be unrestrained as the wind, while carrying the Message of Him Who hath caused the Dawn of Divine Guidance to break. Consider, how the wind, faithful to that which God hath ordained, bloweth upon all regions of the earth, be they inhabited or desolate."

Gl-339

The Bahá'í teacher must do as Bahá'u'lláh said. Be like the wind and it blows wherever and whenever God wills. Desolation or populated areas neither pains nor pleases it.

The story of Jamal Effendi was told to me by some of the friends in India.

One need only look at Jamal Effendi to see how this works and take into consideration the time of plowing, the time of planting, the time of watering, the time of harrowing and the time of harvesting.

Jamal Effendi was sent to India by Bahá'u'lláh and he worked and he worked and he prayed and he prayed. Finally, he gave up and returned to Bahá'u'lláh.

'Abdu'l-Bahá was sitting in the tea house outside Bahjí with some pilgrims. Suddenly he raised his head and said,

"O the fragrance! O the fragrance!" and he rushed out into the road to find Jamal Effendi returning from India. Jamal Effendi asked to be taken to Jamal Mubarak (The Blessed Beauty). When he was ushered into the Divine Presence, he threw himself at the feet of Bahá'u'lláh and through his tears told him that He had sent the wrong man to India. Bahá'u'lláh picked him up and laughed and said I have sent the right man to India. You go back to India.

This time, upon Jamal Effendi's return he found and enrolled that wonderful and dedicated soul Mustafa Rumi, Hand of the Cause of God. They travelled and taught together. Mustafa Rumi then went on to Sri Lanka, Indonesia, Malaysia and as far away as the Philippines. He enrolled and taught 'Abdu'l-Bahá's village of Daidenow so named because it was the first Bahá'í village in Burma. The place where the casket for the remains of the Báb were made.

Now let us move up to the last few years of the Guardians Ten Year Crusade. In India the National Spiritual Assembly was distraught. The end was fast approaching and the goals were still unwon. Someone suggested sending a teaching team to the area that Jamal Effendi first went to. This time whole villages accepted the Cause and asked the Bahá'í teachers where had they been as their fathers and grandfathers had told them that the Bahá'ís were coming.

We have heard over the last 30 years of mass teaching that it is a waste of time and money and the results are not there. When we started teaching in South Carolina one half of one percent of the American Bahá'í Community was black. As I write this over 30% of this Community is black and the largest number of Bahá'ís in America outside of California (which has a large population of Persians) is South Carolina. We must remember that in the realm of the Spirit there is no time. Yet we become frustrated when we don't see the immediate results.

As I was born into a Bahá'í family and at that time the only Bahá'is in Montana were a Mr. Wolcott and my mother and father in Butte, Montana. The nearest Bahá'í to them lived in Spokane, Washington. The next Bahá'ís were in Seattle and then a few in Portland, Oregon and that was all the Bahá'ís in the entire Northwest. A few years ago I attended a state convention for just Northwest Washington and there were over 1500 Bahá'ís registered. This has taken place in just my life time so please dear friends do not think that your precious plowing or planting today will not bring forth an abundant harvest. Your love and obedience in following the instructions will bear fruit into the far distant reaches of time.

So my beloved reader, I truly hope that I have gotten the message across to you. All you have to do is read, try to understand and make an effort. The secret of teaching, of living and of life itself is in the secret of:

FOLLOW THE INSTRUCTIONS

ABBREVIATIONS OF BOOK TITLES

ADJ	.....	Advent of Divine Justice
BA	.....	Bahá'í Administration
BP	.....	Bahá'í Prayers
BWF	.....	Bahá'í World Faith
DAL	.....	Divine Art of Living
DH	.....	Delight of Hearts
FV	.....	Four Valleys
Gl	.....	Gleanings
HWA	.....	Hidden Words (Arabic)
HWP	.....	Hidden Words (Persian)
KA	.....	Kitáb-i-Aqdas
KI	.....	Kitáb-i-Íqán
LG	.....	Lights of Guidance
PP	.....	Priceless Pearl
PT	.....	Paris Talks
SAB	.....	Selections from the Writings of 'Abdu'l-Bahá
SDC	.....	Secrets of Divine Civilization
SV	.....	Seven Valleys
TAB	.....	Tablets of 'Abdu'l-Bahá
TB	.....	Tablets of Bahá'u'lláh
TDP	.....	Tablets of the Divine Plan
WG	.....	Wellspring of Guidance

www.ingramcontent.com/pod-product-compliance
Lightning Source LLC
Chambersburg PA
CBHW020859090426
42736CB00008B/427

9 780976 278061